THEY'RE IN SOME KIND OF FABULOUS NEW CAHOOTS.

P·O·W·E·R
PARTNERS

◆

How Two-Career Couples Can Play to Win

◆

JANE HERSHEY CUOZZO

AND

S. DIANE GRAHAM

MASTERMEDIA LIMITED

NEW YORK

Published by MasterMedia Limited

MASTERMEDIA and colophon are registered trademarks of
MasterMedia Limited.

10 9 8 7 6 5 4 3 2 1

Library of Congress Cataloging-in-Publication Data

Cuozzo, Jane Hershey.
    Power partners: how two-career couples can play to win/by Jane
Hershey Cuozzo and S. Diane Graham.
        p. cm.
    ISBN 0-942361-17-2
    1. Work and family.   2. Dual-career families.   3. Career
development.   I. Graham, S. Diane.   II. Title.
HD4904.25.C86   1990
306.87—dc20   90-35139
                                                       CIP

Designed by Stanley S. Drate/Folio Graphics Co., Inc.

Manufactured in the United States of America

*Jane dedicates this book to her husband,
Steve, who suggested, pushed, edited,
cajoled, kibbitzed, brainstormed, and
best of all . . . believed.*

*Diane dedicates this book to her
encouraging and supportive husband, Terry
Robertson, and their wonderful and unique
children, Todd, Mark, Joshua, Cody, Ashley,
and Cholly Cassandra.*

ACKNOWLEDGMENTS

Power Partners wouldn't have been possible without uncompromising help and enthusiasm from the following people:

- Our publisher, Susan Schiffer Stautberg, who brought us together, and whose energy inspired and amazed us.
- Dr. Shirley Zussman, who gave freely of her wisdom and years of experience, and bestowed confidence and understanding.
- Letitia Baldrige, Dr. Ann Curtain Ward, Dr. Peter G. Hanson, and others who were especially generous with their outstanding insights.
- The managers, public relations representatives, personal assistants, and contacts who made easy work of difficult arrangements.
- MasterMedia's dedicated staff, who put up with our endless requests . . . and always came through.
- The incredible couples herein who opened up their lives and invited us to learn from their lessons in partnership. Marriage will be even better tomorrow because people like yourselves work and love together today.

CONTENTS

◆

· 3 ·

Facing your public together. Coping with the media,
sudden fame, and envy from the competition.

· 4 ·

The dos and don'ts of powerful home entertaining.
When and how to mix business contacts with friends.
Controlling the social thermostat. Working a room
together.

· 5 ·

The hidden power of family life. When the children
come first . . . and when they don't. Setting the best
priorities for you.

· 6 ·

Special problems facing co-preneurs. Why marriages
can teeter when the going is good as well as bad. How
much time together is too much. The importance of
delegation. Discovering each other's complementary
strengths. Evaluating your levels of commitment.

· 7 ·

How sudden (or even gradual) prosperity can erode a
marriage. Access bartering—keeping the bullies in line.
Road warrior risks—releasing travel tensions at home
and away. Learning to live with success.

· 8 ·

PREFACE

Diane Graham and I have different lives. My husband and I reside in a one-bedroom Manhattan apartment. Each of us spends most working days sitting in front of a computer screen—myself at home, Steve at his newspaper office. Even without children, there never seems to be quite enough time to get everything done. Even during the most hassle-packed days, we constantly pinch ourselves, feeling lucky to have found the right person on the first time out.

Diane and her husband, Terry, are the proud parents of six children. Diane runs her own successful multi-million-dollar engineering and technology company in which Terry plays a pivotal role. Their lives are amplified by their spirituality and philanthropic interests, flowing from their gracious Kansas City home and ever-hectic corporate headquarters. Each having been married previously, they, too, feel blessed to have found each other.

What we have in common is our feelings about marriage and partnership. We feel loved and productive—so do our spouses. Is this so unusual?

Many books and articles we've read would lead us to believe that men and women don't (or even want to) fulfill mutual needs or understand each other's points of view. Maybe these authors went looking for negative news. Misery still grabs headlines and commands space on the supermarket racks. And much of it is, unfortunately, unquestionably genuine.

But we know, from our own experiences, that there's a better way to go when it comes to relating and caring. As we began to talk with our own friends and family members, quiet revelations emerged. We aren't alone out there with our supportive spouses who take time to listen and help us see the light.

When the idea of Power Partners came up, some couples insisted, "That's not really us—we're not that strong—our jobs aren't that important. All we do is sit down each evening and talk about how work is going or what we might do to give our ambitions a chance to fly." It was a highly encouraging start.

As we commenced the long and fascinating interviewing process, we became more firmly convinced that for every married couple on the brink of domestic doldrums, another was working themselves *out* of personal and professional ruts.

Some of the couples you'll meet in this book are household names and faces. Others are business and community leaders whose companies' products and services are in many of our own homes. Other pairs are less wealthy and well known—though just as rich in dedication and determination to make the most of their opportunities. These are individuals who encompass a wide range of ethnicities and faiths. Some have lived in the same town in the same state for all of their married life. Many have made at least one major geographical move on account of a partner's career needs. Several go about their work and family raising under two or more roofs.

Some surprises. Most of the wives did not feel particularly guilty about continuing their careers with small children at home. Perhaps this is because most of the men were willing, if not eager, to participate actively in everything from diapering to drug and sex education. No one looked upon raising children as an extension of housework. So much for fast-trackers with neglected kids. These parents really care.

A few visible and famous women, all of whom had made

their professional bones *before* their current marriages, would not participate for fear of spousal disapproval. A common line of decline: "I want to talk about our relationship, but my husband is afraid of what might happen if we go public." Another favorite withdrawal: "If you're happy and talk about it, then something terrible will happen. Who knows? We might break up by the time the book comes out." These phrases came from the mouths of women whose faces and opinions grace TV shows and magazine pages with regularity. Perhaps they had the good inner sense to doubt their own Power Partnership capacity. Maybe we'll have the chance to try again. Maybe their marriages will still be going strong—we hope so.

The men were just as excited and opinionated about our co-mentoring concept as their mates. Singer-songwriter Nick Ashford of Ashford & Simpson told us that he had never been asked such thoughtful questions. What was supposed to be a forty-minute session turned into nearly two hours of introspection. Jim Schroeder, Congresswoman Pat Schroeder's equally dedicated and busy husband, had as much to say about the changing workplace and child-rearing as his frontline wife. High-ranking executives admitted that certain aspects of equal partnership at home and in the office still scared them. Co-preneurs spoke with pride about finding new career opportunities thanks to their spouses' ingenuity and motivation. Fear and trepidation do exist, but so does a distinct willingness to try harder.

Power Partners is not a book that offers magical answers. Real couples do not inhabit landscapes with talking animals and mist-shrouded castles. There aren't many fairy godbosses or children who find rubies in their jeans, either. The married pairs within these pages are moving forward on wings of trial and error. Their innovative momentum will shape relationships into the next century. We believe that their lifestyles can work wonders today. Power to those who have succeeded, and even more to those who keep trying.

—Jane Hershey Cuozzo

POWER PARTNERS

INTRODUCTION: LOVING WISELY AND WELL

Most of us have watched a game of singles tennis. Two individuals in pristine white stand on opposite sides of a net and use every turn of the body and brain to score against one another. No teamwork, no mutual support.

But if you've studied a game of mixed doubles, where a man and a woman work together to outplay the competition, the sport takes on a unique dimension of cooperation and strategy.

He may have a stronger forehand, but display weakness at rushing the net. She may lack a dynamic service, but possess a superior ability to place the ball. Not only can each player compensate for the other's shortcomings, but they can combine skills to create a better game plan.

Like our pair on the court, two-career couples often find it challenging to switch from solo to tandem tournaments. Yet today's dual-income relationships offer each member an opportunity to discover a meaningful and exciting power— the power that lies untapped in most marriages—the power to help each other win at work without losing at home.

We've seen the endless stream of TV news segments and magazine articles on Marriage *à la* M.B.A. This is where the husband and wife run their relationship along the lines of IBM. Perhaps you've met such a couple—the kind who draw up weekly contracts scheduling everything from chimney cleaning to childbirth. Intimacy and interaction are squeezed in between aerobics and selecting a new car stereo.

But compulsive planning rarely leads to personal or professional fulfillment any more than overtraining leads to winning tournaments. These couples have become too focused on individual gains and aspirations. They haven't learned the important difference between being competitors and Power Partners.

Power Partners don't work at finding time for each other. They know instinctively that togetherness builds success. They never demand, "What's in it for me?" Instead, they concentrate on what's mutually advantageous.

Take Deborah Freund and Tom Kniesner, economists on the faculty at Indiana University at Bloomington. Both are highly regarded, but Deborah's specialty, health care delivery, requires frequent travel, giving her more access beyond the academic world than Tom, whose scholarly research and work as a textbook author tends to keep him closer to their campus base. While Deborah was being wooed by a score of prestigious colleges, she began to realize that she had the power to enhance her husband's career as well as her own.

"Tom, whose specialty is labor markets, made me realize how I could use this situation to *both* our advantages. I started to 'sell' ourselves as a team, showing how each of us could increase the strength of the entire institution. Tom's worked at high levels in Washington, D.C., but he just doesn't get the travel opportunities I do." Later, when both of them became disenchanted with their former posts in the East, it was Tom who got headhunted first, and made his contacts aware of Deborah's expertise.

In the pages ahead, you'll meet Power Partners with different careers and goals like Robert and Barbara Taylor Bradford, Ashford & Simpson, and Judy Licht and Jerry Della Femina. You'll also encounter married co-preneurs like shoe biz moguls Joan and David Helpern, jewelers Angela and Bruce Cummings (who did more than breakfast at Tiffany's!), and Ted and Joyce Rice, who've got everyone hot for their T. J. Cinnamons rolls.

There's also a pair of lawyers in love who changed the way their high-profile firm looked at partnerships of a different kind, and several new-style political power teams like Charles and Lynda Robb who dare to break with traditional roles and images.

It isn't always easy to step up to Power Partnering even if the baseline relationship is solid. Many men continue to harbor feelings of anger and inadequacy when their wives end up with higher salaries and superior titles. Conversely, some women may still feel that tug of sisterhood guilt when turning to a husband for help. Even mutual success doesn't guarantee a life of happily ever after. A surprising number of couples find their hard times beginning just as the bank account starts to swell.

But for those who adopt the Power Partner attitude, the rewards can more than compensate for any initial trepidation.

A POWER PARTNER'S PERSONAL COMMANDMENTS

As with all games worth playing, this one has some important ground rules. Consider them laws to live, work, and play by:

1. *Thou Shalt Respect Thy Partner's Goals.* It's a good idea to evaluate the way you honestly feel about day care management, cosmetology, organic farming, or, for that matter, corporate law, advertising, or broadcast journalism. You both must come to terms with any negative attitudes. While it's certainly possible to love, honor, and marry someone without appreciating his or her chosen line of work, you'll never become an effective Power Partner unless you hold your beloved's career in as high esteem as your own.
2. *Thou Shalt Provide Access to Each Other's Contacts.*

Do you know someone at your office who would be perfect to advise your husband on his magazine start-up? Is your new boss on the board of your wife's hospital? Why not bring them together? The operational word here is "timing." Do some subtle digging into the situation and make a move . . . carefully.

3. *Thou Shalt Convert Envy into Energy.* Instead of drawing a bead on your wife's quotes in *USA Today*, focus instead on how her publicity blitz can be parlayed to your benefit. How pleasant—and pro- ductive—to network on board her company's Gulf- stream instead of wrangling with Eastern Airlines. A sudden spurt of fortune for one should be seen as a boon for both!

4. *Thou Shalt Play Fair.* How far should you go to aid an ambitious mate? Brush up your Shakespeare before urging an unethical stratagem. You may not believe that sabotaging your spouse's marketing competitor or planting nasty items about your hus- band's restaurant rival can boomerang (or be traced back to the source). Remember, Lady Macbeth thought she was being supportive, too.

5. *Thou Shalt Learn About Thy Spouse's Business.* Too often couples would like to help with each other's career roadblocks, but feel stymied by an informa- tion gap. It's amazing how little most of us know about our bedmate's business. You won't need to transform yourself into a walking textbook of arbi- trage or astrophysics, but you will have to ask ques- tions. It won't hurt.

6. *Thou Shalt Keep Thy Game Plans Private.* Unless you must, don't share your plans for the future. Inti- macy can only serve to enhance your co-mentoring experience. If you tell the world, sooner or later someone else will be using your best shots.

7. *Thou Shalt Take Time Out from the Tournament.* What's the sense of having a better life if there's no

time to enjoy it? Shrewd Power Partners know that smelling the roses, especially if they're blooming on the lawn of your fully paid for weekend retreat, is as rewarding as having the money to buy them. Whether your indulgences run to Château Margaux or center court seats at the U.S. Open, give yourselves regular treats. Do it in proportion, but don't let a significant raise or promotion go by without some meaningful splurge.

8. *Thou Shalt Not Take the Name of Thy Partner in Vain.* This is advice that's too often ignored until too late in the game. The Public (and public means anything from a cocktail party at home to a White House press conference) is no place to air personal problems. This means no "affectionate" remarks about your husband's personal hygiene habits or your wife's unspeakable second cousin. When you're on-stage together, it doesn't matter who forgot to call the accountant or walk the mastiff. This goes triple if the cameras are rolling or the microphone is live. How different things might have been if Geraldine Ferraro and her spouse had agreed in advance to praise a little more and kibbitz a whole lot less.

9. *Thou Shalt Set Aside Regular Practice Sessions.* Forget those endless tickler lists. Set aside regular weekly or monthly times for long-term planning and practice. No children or VCRs allowed. If necessary, hide out at a hotel.

Sound familiar? It should to anyone who has attended a professional think tank. Companies spend fortunes to sequester executives to ensure undivided attention.

During these sessions, try out other proven methods of problem-solving. Scenarios, brainstormings, and even breakfast meetings can be rebuilt for two. This is the time to be both candid and creative.

Don't waste time with nitpicking—work toward reaching mutually satisfying solutions. If your husband lacks confidence in public speaking, develop remedies that won't crush his ego. Perhaps your firm offers tactical communications courses. Find out if spouses can participate. Offer to go along. Chances are you'll both profit from improved skills, not to mention from meeting new people!

10. *Thou Shalt Put Thy Partner Before Thy Winnings.* Never allow professional aggressiveness to overtake your marriage. The goal here is a team win. If one of you wants a temporary breather, don't feel betrayed. Find out the reasons and see if the change can be made without too much financial or social disruption. Listen to the desires behind the words. As with other adaptations that come with a committed relationship, you may both gain from one partner's personal pause.

These are just the basics for becoming successful Power Partners. You must adapt these rules to suit your own marital style. Some couples' idea of getting ahead is to start a business together. Others envision a life blessed with enough money and flexibility to combine active careers with more family time. And there are those who continue to dream about sailing around the world on an eighty-foot yacht.

Ponder those commandments again. Can you and your spouse identify with at least three of them? Do the dilemmas they raise sound familiar? Now take a look at the following situations. Circle A, B, or C depending on which answer is closest to the way you would respond. Then, have your partner do the same. Remember, there are no *right* or *wrong* answers—but some are more powerful than others!

1. You're meeting someone for the first time at a social occasion. He or she asks what your spouse does for a living. Your answer is most like:
   A. He (she) works in sales.

B. He (she) heads up a sales team for a sporting goods company.

C. He (she) is the vice president of sales for the Acme Tennis Corporation.

2. Today's *Wall Street Journal* features a flattering interview with you and a negative profile of your spouse's company. Your first reaction is to:

   A. Write a hostile letter to the editor.

   B. Book a self-congratulatory dinner at an expensive restaurant.

   C. Call your spouse at work to gauge the mood.

3. Your spouse tells you over dinner that a surefire route to promotion at Topeka's biggest accounting firm is to engage one of your public relations clients to give the keynote address at the annual meeting. The first words to spill from your lips are:

   A. "I can't promise, but I'll certainly bring it up. Give me something I can show Senator Kassebaum to get her interested."

   B. "Don't ever ask me to do something so unprofessional!"

   C. "Does your boss know I represent Senator Kassebaum? Is that why they've put you in charge of finding a speaker?"

4. You've just gotten an unexpected cash bonus equal to a month's salary. The first thing you do on your lunch hour is to:

   A. Spend the entire amount on a home entertainment system.

   B. Lock up the whole bonus in a two-year CD.

   C. Deposit the money in your joint checking account and buy a bottle of vintage wine.

5. The two of you are about to leave for a two-week
   vacation in Europe. The day before your flight, his/
   her boss calls an unscheduled meeting that your
   spouse is expected to attend. You suggest which of
   the following courses:
   A. That your spouse explain the predicament and
      find out the nature of the meeting.
   B. That your spouse should offer to stay for the
      meeting if the company will pick up the airline
      cancellation expenses and add some extra time
      off.
   C. That your spouse simply ignore the meeting—
      after all, the boss knows about the vacation and
      wouldn't schedule anything important without
      saying so in advance.

6. You haven't made love for almost two weeks because
   of work and family hassles. At last, the kids are
   pillow fighting at the neighbor's house and there's
   no report due tomorrow. Just as you're getting into
   the mood, the phone rings. The voice on the answering machine is the Big Client from Kyoto. Do you:
   A. Stop caressing and reach for the receiver.
   B. Reach for the receiver but keep on cuddling.
   C. Laugh and take time out just long enough to
      make sure Mr. Big leaves his number.

7. It's time for the annual holiday open house at your
   place. You discover that one of your invited guests
   has been trouncing your spouse's boss in the local
   papers. Besides removing all sharp objects from the
   living room, you:
   A. Try and steer your potentially troublesome guest
      into safer social waters by introducing her to
      people with similar interests.
   B. Take a deep breath and trust to the spirit of the
      season.

C. Bring the hostile forces together in the hopes that they'll make peace.

8. Your presence is required (not requested) by your spouse at a major awards dinner where he/she is the awardee. You stumble into the ballroom an hour late, having missed the domestic champagne, the rubber shrimp appetizer, and your beloved's acceptance speech. As you slink into the seat at your partner's side, will his/her first words be:
   A. "Did you get the contract?"
   B. "This means it's your turn to serve breakfast in bed for a month!"
   C. "It's a good thing they videotaped me, otherwise you'd be hearing from my lawyer in the morning."

9. Daughter Sally's theatrical debut as a singing donut takes place on the same afternoon as your quarterly report presentation and your spouse's first meeting with the new company director. Seven-year-old Sally refuses to go onstage unless one of you is there. Tossing a coin is definitely out. Your solution is to:
   A. Ask your spouse to lie to his/her boss and show up.
   B. Fib to your company and show up.
   C. Call favorite Auntie Mame to come to the rescue and later take everyone out to Sally's favorite spaghetti house for a big celebration dinner.

10. The *Chicago Tribune* treats you better than Lois Lane and Brenda Starr. You're making a terrific salary, have wonderful perks and benefits, and are less than two years away from being fully vested. Guess who's just been offered the presidency of the new Los Angeles office of Tasti Foods?
    A. You take a deep breath and thank God that you failed the E.P.T. test.

B. Admit to yourself that you've been in a promotion rut, that you hate down coats, and that it would be great to live nearer to all those old buddies from UCLA.

C. Just say NO!

Got the feeling that you've been here before? According to the Conference Board's Work and Family Information Center, of the 55 million working women in this country, half are married to working men—and 25 percent of those 55 million women are managers. That's double the 1972 figure!

Life in the fast track is too tough to go it alone anymore. That doesn't mean sitting back and letting your spouse lob your job shots for the next decade. What it does mean is that it's time to warm up more than the other side of the bed. In the pages ahead, you'll discover men and women who've made the conscious decision to do more for their mates than simply cheer from the sidelines. *Power Partners* demonstrates why these individuals advance more quickly in the workplace, and how you can master their best moves.

The first chapter, "Sizing Up the Court," will help you to evaluate the current state of your marriage and discover how to trade traditional outlooks for fresh cooperative strategies.

Later, you'll learn how to build on your new-found teamwork through mutual networking and other advancement techniques that aren't just for the office anymore.

Some of the world's most famous and successful couples will share their personal (and surprisingly universal) moments of triumph and setback. Access to limos, nannies, and dependable dry cleaners can help, but not as much as a savvy and sympathetic spouse whose eye is focused as firmly on your career goals as his or her own.

America's leading women's fashion designer, Donna Karan, and sculptor/business partner spouse, Stephan Weiss, have taken this approach to heart. Says Karan, "Being in such a career-oriented lifestyle, it's essential to share goals and visions. Stephan and I understand what each of us is going through and that brings us closer together."

You'll see how one partner copes when the other moves ahead at a faster pace, or springs a sudden change. Find out how today's most dynamic duos combine business with more pleasurable pursuits . . . like power entertaining and vacationing. Public relations whiz Linda Robinson, wife of American Express CEO and chairman James Robinson III, and Laurie Johnson, spouse to former RJR Nabisco chairman Ross Johnson (and vice president of their RJM Group consulting firm), talked their partners into taking a Greek cruise together. One assumes that the quartet came back with more than good tans and an appreciation for ancient ruins!

As children, we were constantly admonished to share. A super ice cream sundae would make one person sick, but two best friends contentedly full. As sundaes turn into cash bonuses, the concept of splitting the spoils becomes more meaningful. Everyone needs a special someone to share the wealth as well as the woes and the work.

This doesn't mean that Power Partners surrender their individuality or personal indulgences. Nor does it mean passing on full responsibility for hits and misses. Ultimately, it's still up to *each of you* to make the system work to the advantage of both.

In closing their joint autobiography, *Unlimited Partners*, Secretary of Labor Elizabeth Dole and her senator husband, Robert, had this to say about their close-knit professional and personal lives:

"Writing a book together has something in common with marriage. If you can't decide who gets the last word, you might as well share it. . . . We may not always have recalled events in the same light, but then, what married couple doesn't occasionally agree to disagree?

"If you think government is full of checks and balances, you should see a dual career between people who love their work second only to each other. Our solution is simple: we share the good times as we share the sacrifices—equally."

You're not going to get the answers to those ten Power Partner scenarios right away. As we said before, *most* of them don't have a single "right" or "wrong" response. Throughout the book, you'll find out how the best Power Partners have handled such situations. You'll also learn what experts like etiquette authority Letitia Baldrige and leading psychotherapist Dr. Shirley Zussman would have selected as their preferred choices. The important point is that you and your partner ponder them together.

Power Partners will not help you resolve serious conflicts in your relationship. Nor can this type of teamwork create a scientific genius or award-winning copywriter if the talent and skills aren't there at the start. Power Partnering entails commitment and effort. But if you and your spouse have a strong sense of what would make your good life together that much better, the next eight chapters can change the good into great . . . that much faster!

Communication will always be the cornerstone of a lively and productive marriage. Becoming a harmonious team will take time, energy, humor, and, above all, constant communication. But even before the mortgage is paid off and the promotions are announced, you'll begin to see a new confidence in yourself and your partner. Just remember that this game, like the one played on the tennis court, always begins with love.

Authors' Note: Throughout the book, the majority of interview subjects are identified by their full names. Certain individuals wished to maintain anonymity for professional reasons. In those particular instances, we have either identified them by first name only, or changed their names to protect their privacy.

1

SIZING UP THE COURT

♦

There is no set formula for a successful marriage. Ask fifty couples about the hows and whys of staying together and the answers will be as diverse as the individuals who make up the partnerships.

Since the beginning of time, marriages have been made practically everywhere *but* heaven. Marriage stabilizes our world. A famous upper-crust eighteenth-century German philosopher summed it up succinctly if a tad coldly when he decreed: "Marriage is to politics what the lever is to engineering. The state is not founded upon single individuals but upon couples and groups."

Not that the couple-craving body politic has always encouraged pairing up for romantic reasons. Even now, royal families match emotionally unprepared scions with selected titled women known more for their child-bearing capabilities than strong opinions. And at less lofty levels some couplings appear at first glance to be based largely on social acceptance and a willingness to live out a prescribed way of life.

However, today more unions are actually being founded on the right stuff—attraction, affection, respect, and eventually love. A lot of that has to do with the fact that growing numbers of men and women are hard at work in environments that inspire a new kind of loving—one that doesn't preclude professional empathy. As a recent *Fortune* magazine article on CEOs' second wives reported, dynamic men don't want women around who can't keep up. And ambitious women don't want to associate with men who expect them to sacrifice their careers for a fancy wardrobe. (Designer Carolyne Roehm made certain she got both in her marriage to leveraged-buyout king Henry Kravis.)

Down from cloud levels on the lifestyle scale, construction workers and cops are getting used to female colleagues on a regular basis. Even rock'n'roll women are more likely to tote the Fender than simply sing backup. Bruce Springsteen married the requisite "model" wife; she was almost immediately kicked off the nuptial stage by his own comely guitarist. Patti Scialfa's extra talent was, no doubt, her ability to identify with her fellow performer's daily problems.

The couples included in this book feel that marriage has changed for the better. Yes, the divorce rate has gone up, but so has the number of marriages. Women are going into their first marriages later than they did in the 1950s and 1960s; they know a bit more about who they are and what they need in a long-term emotional relationship. Most of the pairs we interviewed met through a professional situation. Either they were working at the same company, or their careers conveniently crossed paths at the right moment.

Margaret Kent, author of *Love at Work*, feels that couples who meet through work have a good start because they are more likely to become friends first. It's easier for them to obtain "inside information" on each other.

A growing number of corporations are learning to accept this trend.

Dar Di Sabatino works for Du Pont as a development and employee relations consultant. Her husband, George Palmer, is also employed by Du Pont, as a public affairs manager. Ironically, the pair did not meet at their common workplace, but found themselves living across the street from each other in the same Delaware community.

They give their company high marks for progressive attitudes toward two-career couples. Says Palmer, "Du Pont has accepted the dual-career marriage, even when both partners work for them. Of course, if someone reported to the other, management would try to make an acceptable adjustment within the corporation, but no one would be penalized."

Adds Di Sabatino, "We've been lucky. Du Pont gives employees a lot of opportunity."

While Sabatino works in the area of employee relations, she actually becomes one of her husband's clients. But even that poses few problems. "Du Pont thinks people should manage their own careers and relationships," says Palmer. "They try and work with the couples as much as possible."

Changes are also occurring in the conservative legal sphere. When Harvey Horowitz, managing partner at New York's prestigious law firm Squadron, Ellenoff, Plesent & Lehrer, met his wife, Eugenie Gavenchak, she was a first-year associate. "When our relationship started getting serious, I thought about letting other partners know that if someone had to leave, it might not be her!" recalls Harvey.

Genie remembers when she first came to the firm in early 1979. "I was really excited about being at a highly visible Manhattan firm with top-notch people. I met Harvey briefly, but that was it. A short time later, we were working together around the clock on an important case."

Harvey and Genie were brought together by the famous disco Studio 54. "The club was about to lose its liquor license. We spent hours at Studio 54 with potential witnesses. Then we'd go back to the office and work together some more. I really came to respect Harvey's legal brilliance, but there was still nothing more than intense camaraderie between us. A month or so after the case had closed, he invited me out to a black-tie benefit at Lincoln Center. Shortly after that, we began to get serious."

The pair decided to go public with their romance when

they moved in together that fall. "I was extremely pleased with everyone's reaction," Genie recalls. "Some of the other partners came into my office and congratulated me!" A few years later, when Harvey and Genie legalized their cohabitation, the firm presented them with a generous wedding gift.

They admit that theirs is still not your typical law firm romance. Monica and Eric, another successful pair of East Coast attorneys, also met at a high-powered New York law office."We were both associates and while we never even saw each other much during the day, we still had to be secretive. It was fun at first, but, later, when we decided to marry, I knew that at least one of us would have to leave." As it turned out, both opted to go. Today, they live in a prosperous New Jersey suburb and have become senior staff lawyers for a major bank and a *Fortune* 500 company.

Genie feels that a lot depends upon the employees themselves. "I always felt comfortable at Squadron. By the time I was up for partnership, I already had the sense I was on the right track. I think that if Harvey and I had to work together all the time, we might have more professional stress in our lives. As it is, we enjoy the occasional case where we share the load. You do take it home with you, but in short spurts, it's fun."

Prudential Insurance is another company that doesn't mind having its employees doubling up under "tasteful" circumstances. As one VP explained, "Quite a few people meet here, get married, and stay on with us. In fact, we've sent people away on training sessions only to have them come home engaged. We have to accept the fact that with so many employees, some difficult office liaisons will occur. But, generally, I think it's healthier to have some flirtation in the air. Prudential likes to recruit bright men and women right out of college and graduate school. It's only natural that young people are on the lookout for someone to love."

Marie-Claude Stockl, senior vice president of Manning, Selvage & Lee, a large public relations firm, has her own view of how companies can best serve intracorporate couples. "The biggest benefit is equal salaries for men and women. My former employer, Bristol-Myers"—where Stockl served as director of public affairs—"gets a good rating in that area. Their human resource department is excellent. They're quite advanced when it comes to things like flex hours and parental leave."

Stockl believes that the toughest problem for two-career spouses is relocation. "You get into whose career is more important. It's crucial to consider why you want to relocate and discuss it thoroughly."

Let's face it—almost everyone's working. When today's men and women marry, it will most likely be to someone who has a full-time occupation. According to a 1989 *New York Times* survey, most married working women continue to feel that their husbands don't help out equally at home when it comes to chores and child care. On the other side of the equality coin, the Bureau of Labor Statistics shows that more women are entering work areas, blue and white collar, that have traditionally been male bastions.

Surely the results will be for men and women to be increasingly drawn toward partners who understand and are possibly intrigued by what each one does for a living. While that hardly sounds like the stuff of moonlight and champagne, it's really not a bad way to evaluate future compatibility. Work is where many of us spend most of our time; there's too little of the latter left to waste it on someone who can't even relate, not to mention help out.

"I can't imagine not understanding what your partner does for a living," says Mary, a marketing director for a prestigious family-run hotel group. "My husband, Richard, is an international real estate developer. Even if we hadn't met when I was in the same business, I would have made it a priority to find out enough about what he did to give him support and advice."

The Power Partner approach requires the presence of a solid marital relationship.

THE COMMUNICATION CONNECTION

Being able to communicate effectively about what you do and having your communications *fully understood* by a spouse are essential for successful two-career coupling.

Novelist Barbara Taylor Bradford, author of the record-breaking best-seller *A Woman of Substance*, nearly always turns first to her husband and business partner, Robert, for feedback on her writing. Here is an illustration of major league Power Partnering at its most successful: not only is Barbara known to millions of loyal readers, but Robert, a veteran producer, has set out the ambitious goal of creating television miniseries of all of her novels, boasting stellar casts including Deborah Kerr and James Brolin. "I'm not a very confiding person," admits Barbara. "When I'm working on a book, Bob is the only one who gets to read anything along the way. He sees the draft before my editor does. I know all about his production plans, too. Not communicating can destroy a marriage."

Real estate developer Richard admits that "I didn't have adequate communications skills in my first marriage. Not having them hurt my business dealings, too. Whatever you do or don't have in your marriage carries over into your work. People rarely communicate as well as they think— you've got to work at getting your messages across."

Communication should also reinforce mutual respect. Not only for each other's professional skills and goals, but for emotional and psychological contributions to the spousal alliance.

Betty Hudson, vice president of corporate and media relations at NBC, speaks with quiet, caring pride about her husband, "USA Today" TV anchor Boyd Matson. "We have a strong, mutual appreciation—more of an ongoing enlightenment than concern over topping one another. I know how hard it is to do what he does."

It's important to ask yourself how you view your spouse's source of income. Evelyn Sherburne, a Pennsylvania school psychologist married to a salesman and distributor for a dried meats company, thinks of her husband's work in terms of his skills.

"When I think of Pat's work, I don't think of *what* but of *how*. Not that he's a beef jerky salesman, but how he manages all those salespeople. How he organizes his time on the road. How he uses his sales ability. He sees me as someone who understands why people act the way they do, and helps rid them of negative reactions which hold them back. It won't matter in the future what either of us does professionally because our mutual respect isn't tied to a single job description."

Evelyn admits that this attitude is easier to foster in their rural community than it might be in her native New York City. But the same game can be played just as effectively on concrete as on grass. Try the following empathizing exercises:

- Imagine yourself at your spouse's workplace. What does it look like? What kinds of problems might you be facing today? What skills will you need to solve them?
- Think about the most critical work decision your partner has had to make this past month. Would he/she agree with your choice?
- The next time your spouse needs professional ego stroking, instead of just reciting anticipated endearments, describe and praise his or her most potent professional strong points.

If you and your spouse are already effective communicators, then you are most likely to be spontaneously using these types of exercises as part of your regular exchange of feelings and ideas. This shows that each of you has accepted the other's career ambitions and preferences as an integral part of the *whole partner*.

EXPECTATIONS

What do you and your spouse *want* from your life together? When you decided to marry, was it really for richer or poorer, better or worse, in sickness and health? Status, money, and glamour aren't bad aphrodisiacs, but getting each other through bad times and unexpected situations takes more than a gold credit card approach to wedded bliss.

A prominent divorce lawyer calls them "maximum efficiency" marriages. These are couples who stay together as long as their careers and public lives flourish. During an interview, one such couple bragged about how much they helped each other's high-wire publishing ventures; when asked about what would happen if one of them became seriously incapacitated or just wanted to give up, the air went dead. "It's simply not in the program," said the man. "I mean, if I became a paraplegic or got Alzheimer's, I'd expect her to provide me with the proper care and get on with her own life."

Dr. Shirley Zussman, a leading New York marital therapist, believes that these marriages *can* work out, but only if the couple starts to care along the way. "If the only basis is mutual excitement over business, then the pair usually drifts, but if they manage to grow into love, they might be good together."

Don't confuse this with taking pleasure in the perks that your or your spouse's occupations might bring. Discounted hotel suites, free concert tickets, and going wholesale are nothing to feel guilty about if they come by way of hard work and achievement. But ask yourself how you would feel if they vanished tomorrow. Would you heave a brief sigh of regret and start regrouping, or would you think seriously about withholding sexual and other personal favors?

What about the roles you assumed that each of you would play when you first linked up? Was there some kind of contract, spoken or unspoken, designating each of you responsible for certain facets of your marriage? Did your husband expect you to work until children arrived, or continue as a full-time careerist? Did your wife know about your ambitions to leave your law firm and set up a storefront practice in a disadvantaged neighborhood? Have you worked out a personal finance plan that you both can live with?

Have you talked about what might happen to your relationship if one or both of you changed professions?

Try acting out the following scenarios. Do this first *without* your spouse's presence. Then, repeat the procedure in front of your husband or wife:

- Your spouse earns enough money to support the household at a comfortable level. Your income enables the family to save and splurge. Even though your job pays less than your spouse's, you are happier in your position than your spouse is at his/her work. Then, one evening, your spouse comes home and announces that he/she has quit.

- For five years, you have done all of the housekeeping and your spouse has done all of the food shopping and preparation. You want to reverse responsibilities for a while. You are bringing the matter up over a gourmet home-cooked dinner.

- You have always believed that a couple should share all personal finances. Now your spouse is trying to convince you that there are good reasons to separate some of your joint assets.

- The two of you are at a party. You head for the buffet to bring back some dessert. As you sit down next to your spouse, you hear him/her say to a new acquaintance, "I've always wanted to breed horses, but guess who would go crazy living in the country."

How hard was it for you and your spouse to resolve these scenes? Did you find yourself giving one response when you tried it alone, and a different set of answers when your partner was present? Did talking out any of these situations lead toward resolution of a conflict in your own life?

If your private responses were vastly different from those made in front of your spouse, perhaps your marriage isn't open enough yet for true Power Partnership. *Honesty* is a critical component for any couple who wishes to take a more aggressive approach to helping each other professionally. Disagreements usually don't herald personal disasters unless one partner or both are dissembling. It's okay to feel guilty, angry, or resentful in a marriage. It's definitely *not okay* to feel that way and never talk about it! Or, worse yet, pretend it doesn't exist.

Photographer and environmental activist Linda McCartney has said that one reason she and Paul have such a strong marriage is that she is able to stand up for herself. "You have to respect yourself. If you don't, you can't expect others to respect you. We all want to make our man happy and sometimes we feel guilty when he isn't. But you have to remember that each person has control over their own lives. It's not your fault. Eventually I explode. Paul likes that. He feels a good row is healthy for a relationship, so long as you make up afterwards."

A FINE ROMANCE

Sex is important. Or should be. But romance is even more vital to anchor an ongoing relationship that's going to be tossed about by periods of upheaval and unpredictability. A touch of the quixotic can do wonders to soften the edges of a grueling workday. A romantic gesture can lead to the bedroom, but that shouldn't always be the final destination. Sharing a fleeting memory of a personal past event can relieve tension during a corporate cocktail party. Finding an unexpected intimate gift waiting at home on a rainy evening helps to reaffirm self-worth. When was the last time you and your partner did one of the following:

- Took a spontaneous weekend break together?
- Bought each other a long-time coveted present *without* waiting for a birthday or holiday?
- Told each other how great it is to be in the other's life?
- Spent time reminiscing about your courtship?

Romance is part of the communication connection. You don't have to be there in the flesh to have your feelings felt.

A cool technological tool can become, with help from a fanciful imagination, a means to a new kind of love letter. Answering machines, especially those that let specified callers leave "secret" messages, can become a romantic ally. One oft-traveling fashion buyer relies on her lawyer husband's "good night faxes" to smile her to sleep on hectic European buying jaunts.

TRUST

The *T* word. We wish it always applied to our business associates, elected officials, clergy, doctors, lawyers, brokers, and children. Sometimes they let us down . . . hard. My boss told me that I was getting that promotion and then she gave it to . . . I think my daughter is lying about where she got that necklace. . . . Why do I feel that my doctor isn't giving me the whole picture?

Power Partners must trust each other . . . completely. Trust doesn't come instantly. It shouldn't. Trust is earned through time and deeds. How many of the following types of trust are always present in your marriage?

- Sexual trust. Not only fidelity, but honesty about sexual history, health, and happiness!
- Emotional trust. When the two of you discuss important personal issues, each of you displays true emotions and feelings, even if the result is temporary friction. You can go through short periods of not liking each other without worrying about a loss of love.
- Professional trust. You can always depend on your spouse for public support. Neither of you would ever sell the other out for personal professional gain.

As one confident second wife put it, "If you trust your husband, then you don't have to worry if things go wrong; you can usually overcome most problems in a marriage if that total security is there. My husband won't talk much yet about his first marriage. I do know that there was a lot of pain and mistrust. Little by little, he's learning that I'm not the same kind of person. I trust him enough already to let him open up at his own pace."

Real estate developer Richard adds, "In the old concept of marriage, trust was largely physical. Now we have the added rules of emotional and business trust. Lots of us learned lessons from the 1960s. The physical is temporal. Not everyone may agree with me, but I think that you can't 'own' each other physically. The big issue for me is emotional trust. Our business perspective comes from that emotional tie."

CAPACITY FOR COPING WITH CHANGE

People *do* change. They change from single to married. They change from students to teachers and sometimes back to students again. They become parents and then grandparents (Mick Jagger is old enough to be one and Ringo *is* one!). Career-minded couples can start climbing their respective ladders at the same pace, and then, suddenly, one will land at the top while the other is still struggling or falling off altogether. These same duos can decide to pull up stakes and relocate, only to find that one of them can't tolerate the new climate (or job).

Economic climates change, too. Couples can fall in love and marry when everything's going their way, only to find that by the second or third anniversary, the market for time shares or tree trimmers has dried up.

Lynda Johnson Robb is a woman who has had to cope with sweeping changes since she was born. This articulate former president's daughter believed that her marriage to Marine officer Charles Robb finally meant an end to life in the political fishbowl.

"We had been married for ten years before Chuck told me that he wanted to serve his country in another way. I tried to dissuade him because I knew he would be compared with my father, Lyndon Johnson. But now he's the senator from Virginia and I'm back in the political arena. You have to be flexible. The worst thing a couple can do is to make iron-clad rules. Chuck and I aren't the same people we were when we got married back in the 1960s. Each of us has had to make some compromises. The key is to change together and balance each other. Marriage is really a 90/10—each one has to compromise 90 percent. You should both accept the fact that there are going to be adjustments of some kind along the way."

COMMITMENT

Unfortunately, a surprising number of couples haven't thought about the extent of their commitment to marriage. Like the partner who wanted his spouse simply to walk away if he became too incapacitated, some couples won't even face the inevitable fact that a deep ravine may exist somewhere down the road. It may be an unexpected firing, a serious illness, or loss of worldly goods. For many couples in these stressful times, it means a troubled child, an addiction to drugs or alcohol, or psychological collapse.

While no one wants to tempt fate, it's important to note how many couples can and do make it through the storms. Those who have weathered major personal challenges often come out ahead in their professional dealings, too. As one woman put it, "Having my company bought by the Japanese was a cinch compared with Jack's heart attack. Everyone else was acting like the world was coming to an end. I told my associates to take time out and put the situation in its proper perspective. As it happened, our new owners have turned out to be far better than expected. Whenever there's a business crisis in my life, I just go back in my mind to the image of my husband lying there stuck full of tubes and thank God! Nothing at work could ever be as vast an emotional commitment as pulling him through. That experience taught both of us a lot about that old 'hidden springs of strength' stuff."

Boyd Matson was removed as a Sunday "Today" show co-anchor while his wife, Betty Hudson, was moving up the corporate ladder at the same network, NBC. Both of them were aware that home tensions were building. "But," he acknowledges, "there was a new baby to feed, and a marriage that came first. Betty offered some of her greatest support just by putting up with me. And that wasn't easy at the time."

There's not much sense in developing each other's professional potential if the payoff isn't going to be more than paycheck deep. *Power Partnering should fortify the entire marriage.* If the depth of commitment isn't there, the occasional cracks in the co-mentoring road could become emotional black holes.

At this point, it's a good idea to give yourself (and your spouse) an honest appraisal. Are you the kind of couple who can agree to disagree over routine matters without calling Jacoby & Meyers? Do you share *more* than strong career drives? Do you trust one another in the areas we've mentioned, or are there still some lingering doubts? How much time and energy is each of you willing to give to help the other achieve his or her professional goals? Can each of you say "I love you" out loud?

If you find that it's easy to "just say yes" to the above, then it's time to move on to the next step in the Power Partnering game.

YOUR PERSONAL MARITAL STYLE

Are you the kind of couple who doesn't care what the neighbors or in-laws think, as long as it works for you? The answer here should be yes. Everyone likes outside approval for their personal actions, but the best marriages trust in the partnership's own individual style.

Follow the Leader

Diane Levbarg-Klein and her husband, Martin, are a successful, work-oriented couple who live some people's idea of a dream life. She sets up the U.S. concessions for famous fashion designers like Givenchy, Dior, and Missoni. Martin, a corporate lawyer, helps work out her intricate contracts and locates real estate for her clients. The pair own property in Palm Beach and New York, and sometimes summer in the South of France. While they consider themselves in business together, Diane states that Martin makes nearly all her personal and social decisions.

"When I became successful, Marty told me I should do charity work. I didn't want to, but I did it because that was the only way to get him to stop telling me to do it. The same goes for what I do professionally. I was at Bloomingdale's and doing extremely well, but my travel schedule was ghastly. Marty wanted me to travel less, so he arranged for me to get the position of setting up Givenchy's New York boutique."

She then went on to say that her husband rarely shares much of his legal dealings at the dinner table. "Once, I opened my mouth about something confidential at the wrong time," she explained.

At first, this relationship appears to be one-sided in terms of both power and partnership. But it's important to remember that Diane freely stated all of this right in front of her husband. It was obvious that there was a heck of a lot more partnership flowing under the surface. Diane admitted that when they got married (her second; his first), she was selfish by nature. "I'm still a terrible sharer," she confessed. "We hated each other the first year." But, in the same breath, she went on to rave about Martin's unlimited supportiveness and romantic sensibility. "I couldn't have gotten through my parents' divorce without his compassion." In turn, Martin admitted that Diane took dominance over their personal calendar. "When I say we're going to that opening, or having dinner with those people, he caves in and comes along. Or at least he'd better!" Levbarg-Klein laughs.

This couple has the kind of relationship where one partner appears to lead and the other to follow. This has worked for the Levbarg-Kleins, who will be celebrating their sixteenth anniversary. The reason their marriage stays strong is that the leading and following has been a mutual decision. Together, this pair has designed a style that suits them both.

It's My Turn

Brenda and Scott Burrows met while attending college in the Detroit area. After getting her degree, Brenda obtained a lucrative position at a respected public relations firm. Scott went on with his first professional love, music. "When we got married, the big decision was moving," recalls Brenda. "At first I felt a bit resentful about having to give up my job and proximity to most of our friends. But I knew that Scott had the talent and drive to make it as a player and composer. There really wasn't any choice for him except New York. We talked it over constantly. Once we made our move, I realized that this really was better for my career, too. After all, what city has more public relations opportunities than the Big Apple?"

Their first year was tough. "I remember feeling slightly sad about our rather dilapidated home in Brooklyn. Most people we knew were saving and spending on their houses and apartments; we put most of our money into musical instruments and a home studio."

Fortunately, their careers are working out well. Brenda is an account supervisor at an established Manhattan PR firm, and Scott has already won a composing award from the Song Writers' Hall of Fame. "Pretty soon it's going to be my turn to have more flexible, risk-taking options. Right now, Scott is working pretty steadily. I've been writing children's books, and we've even started working on a musical together," says Brenda.

Brenda is not resentful about her husband's career path. "I knew that developing his musical reputation was going to take time. We have so many other things in common that it's nice to have different professional paths. People at work aren't permanent. If you go through your working years living for nothing else, you end up with precious little. I really enjoy the life we have right now. Even if we do strike

it rich someday, it won't change us that much. We'd probably use the money to produce our musical and buy a lot of
nice gifts for our families."

Balancing Acts

"Our first year of marriage was spent largely on building
up our respective businesses." That no-nonsense statement
was made by a vibrant blonde named Lauren Falk. Lauren
and her husband, Michael, run their own successful businesses out of Bloomfield Hills, Michigan. They even have
their own publicity director. Lauren is the editor of *RTW*, a
fashion industry newsletter, while Michael is the president
of Marketing Strategies Group, Inc., servicing clients like
Pepsi-Cola (his former employer) and Domino's Pizza.

Although barely into their thirties, Lauren and Michael
have already made nationwide names for themselves in their
chosen fields. Michael described their marriage as a case of
classic team spirit. "I took the first financial risk toward
independence when Lauren had a steady retail position.
Soon, she followed me onto the entrepreneurial trail. We're
now in the amazingly fortunate position of having two separate but equally fruitful enterprises under one roof."

Lauren stresses that it's their deeply felt bond of love
and respect that keeps their business drives at full tilt.
"Some couples make good professional teams, but I think
we have a special closeness. I can talk to Michael about
anything. We couldn't work as hard if we weren't in love.
There's no separation in our business and personal lives.
Everything we earn and achieve is for *us*. We get real pleasure from seeing us both succeeding."

ORGANIZATION: ANOTHER ELEMENT OF STYLE

Do you and your spouse take comfort in making plans
together? Are you happier knowing Saturday's agenda by
noon on the preceding Monday? Do you enjoy making the
party decorations for your daughter's luau, even though it

cuts into your afternoon golf game? At work, do you look forward to calling staff meetings?

In contrast, are you and your beloved the kind of folks who relish the thought of unplanned weekends? Are there party planners in your future? Does the phrase "five years from now" make your palms sweat?

Couples who answer yes to the first set of questions are Where and Wheners. They are at their most secure when they focus ahead of time on what's down the road. They tend to be outwardly social and get a strong ego boost from doing rather than delegating.

Partners who answer in the affirmative to the questions in the second paragraph are Here and Nowers. These people cringe at the concept of making long-standing dates, and take no personal pleasure in baking one's own bread for brunch if there's a four-star bakery nearby. They can be highly dynamic during the moment at hand—just don't ask them what they're doing New Year's Eve as they bask in the August sun.

Most likely you and your mate fit in somewhere between these two extremes. It's good to have a handle on your organizational style before you begin the co-mentoring process in earnest. Otherwise, you'll find yourself trying out techniques that won't end up working for you.

MONEY MATTERS

Like sex, it certainly does. Potential Power Partners have to agree on a financial style that's suitable for both of them. While Dr. Zussman and others feel that couples who refuse to share *any* personal assets may be less successful at long-term marital commitment, this system can work for some couples—the operative words here are "honesty" and "support." Is each of you being honest about your reasons for keeping everything his and hers? Do you share anything else in your relationship (property, furnishings, dividends)? Are you both equally secure with this system?

A more common approach is one in which the couple

shares major assets like property, investment portfolios, and savings instruments, but keeps individual "mad money" checking accounts. The idea here is that each partner gives the other "permission" to use a set portion of the family money pot on self-indulgent impulses. Some men and women find this adds to marital romance, since they can "treat" their respective partners, much in the same way as during their dating days.

Just as common is the system in which everything belongs jointly to both partners. Revisions in many state divorce laws are making this concept easier for even second- and third-time-around marrieds to live with. The majority of the couples in this book fell into this category.

In her book *Love and Money*, author Carol Colman asserts that "while you don't always have the control over whether you get a raise or get laid off, you *do* have the power to control your own personal financial situation. . . . Often it's not the amount of money a couple has that determines financial security, it's how well they manage it; and that goes back to their relationship."

Another crucial money-related question you should ask yourselves involves the relative size of individual earnings. In plain English, will it bother you if one partner makes significantly more or less? Men are traditionally the ones who tend to find this a loaded question. But with today's rapidly increasing number of high-earning female spouses, women had better check their own bottom line egos.

Whatever your marital money style, make certain that it satisfies both of you in equal measure. Power Partners can't afford the losses accrued through bad feelings about the bedroom or balance sheet.

THE FRIENDSHIP FACTOR

Hackneyed but true, the best Power Partners consider their spouses to be "best friends," too. We heard this over and over, along with the word "team." Just as with anyone else you'd do business with, or would decide to co-mentor, you'd better like them . . . a lot!

Is it possible to *love* someone and not *like* them? Dr. Zussman believes that it can happen in some marriages. "These couples spend time together only when their traditional married roles call for it. They don't think of each other as primary confidants and companions. It's difficult for them to share work experiences because they're not terribly interested in each other's lives outside the confines of the domestic arena. Eventually, this avoidance leads to stagnation of the relationship in all areas."

Think about how much time you and your spouse spend in each other's company when you're not engaged in one of the following:

- Sex
- Child care
- Household chores and decisions

If given the choice, would you want to spend at least 50 percent of your leisure time with your husband or wife? How many outside interests do you *really* share? Has each of you made at least *one effort* to learn more about a sport, hobby, or subject that intrigues your mate? Eleanor Raynolds, CBE, a partner at the executive search firm of Ward Howell International, feels that all couples should have "projects."

"My husband, John (president of Outward Bound), and I built a house together. Doing something that's removed from your regular routine is relaxing and helps you to uncover each other's hidden talents." The pair has also written a book about volunteerism, *Beyond Success: How Volunteer Service Can Help You Begin Making a Life Instead of Just a Living*.

These so-called "projects" need not be that ambitious. Is there a skill both of you have been itching to learn? Get a brochure from your local college or YMCA. Most adult education programs are low-cost and have flexible schedules. Maybe you want to learn piano and your husband wants to play the cello. It's still music. And sharing your "homework" might help you tune up other areas of your professional and personal lives.

Taking part in meditative activities together can also create strong marital bonds. Eleanor Raynolds says, "Religion plays a very big role in our lives. We go to church nearly every Sunday. Our spiritual life is important to us. We feel a higher power meant for us to meet. We're very fortunate."

She continues. "Having the same faith can be an enormous plus. But even if you have different beliefs, you can share the powerful silence of prayer."

Couples who like each other tend to meet new people more easily. As you will see in the chapters to come, this is a highly valuable accomplishment. These people always make time for each other. No matter how hectic the home or office situation becomes, spouses who like being together always find a way to do so . . . even if it means letting the bills sit for one more day, or staying an extra hour on Friday to keep the weekend free for an overnight canoe trip.

Once you've discovered the special, unique qualities that make your marriage different from your mother's, brother's, or best buddy's, you should begin to feel a deepening bond between you. Just as elephants have a low-frequency language that no other species can hear, couples who like and love each other develop private lines of communication. Words, gestures, and expressions that hold neutral importance for everyone else become secret passwords of intimacy, conveying reassurance and good feelings across a room or a continent. Many couples actually swear that they can read each other's thoughts. This isn't magic or ESP—it's the results of a strong relationship.

PARTNERS FOR THE POSITIVE

We live in a highly defensive society. The word "against" floods our media. Women Against Rape. Mothers Against Drunk Drivers. The Fight Against Drugs. These three "againsts" are good ones. But this toughness shouldn't diminish the nurturing, beneficial aspects of today's life. AIDS has made a hellish case for sexual caution, but that fear must not carry over into the bedrooms of monogamous, caring couples. Similarly, recent disregard for fair play on Wall Street does not mean that there's a Gordon Gekko lurking behind every dollar-wise deal. We must all be more careful and perhaps a bit less generous with that aforementioned *T* word. Less generous, but no less faithful.

These are the best of times to begin a Power Partnership. We are shifting away from the "me" to the "us" generation. The borders between the workplace and home are beginning to blend in earnest, thanks to a still-sluggish but increasing trend toward co-preneuring. We are learning that children will not wilt at the sight of Daddy *and* Mommy going to an office if there's security and caring in the air. And most of us are ready to admit that a healthy marriage means making an effort . . . every day.

If we're going to work harder at our chosen professions *and* our most sacred of intimate alliances, then why not merge all that effort? A marriage that's in good shape can take a surprising amount of bending and stretching. Taking your goals to the point of no return is only dangerous when there's no place to return to if they should fall short. Ellie Raynolds puts it like this: "When you are well situated as a couple, you don't have fear. That frees each of you to be more of a professional risk-taker."

The amount of risk is up to the two of you. A great many couples are already Power Partners in spirit if not deed. Do your spouse's career accomplishments make you feel good about yourself? Do your children and other intimates see you as individuals who slip easily in and out of multiple roles? Are you both at your happiest when you're helping each other achieve? All of these reflect a Power Partnership outlook.

The next chapter will start you toward setting up a strong co-mentoring model. As we've already cautioned, none of this is a substitute for talent and industry. Some of these techniques may even add temporary stress to your relationship. That's why we encourage you to examine your marriage openly.

If you feel that you and your spouse aren't ready for a complete Power Partner offensive, don't despair. It's okay to start slowly. And remember—there are no pat answers or single-dimension solutions.

Even if the following chapters serve only to get you and your spouse to deal more dynamically with each other . . . that's a major step forward. For couples with the courage to walk hand in hand onto the field, playing this game can lead to the biggest win of all.

2

CREATING A PERSONAL PLAYSTYLE

◆

Creating an effective Power Partnering routine takes time, patience, and daring. Some of the ideas you'll find in this chapter may appear bold and unorthodox—but so are today's best business strategies. You are about to restructure your relationship in an entirely new and powerful way.

No one expects you and your partner to incorporate every component of this co-mentoring plan. Some of what follows may not sit comfortably with your particular marital style; you and your spouse should read through this chapter together. Then decide where you both want to start making your first changes. Whatever the two of you decide to tackle first, promise each other that you'll stick to it for at least six months. It's important not to take on more than you can handle or to set yourselves unrealistic deadlines for tangible results. Good luck, and may *both* partners win!

RESPONSE REACTIONS: OUT WITH THE OLD

Remember those commandments from the Introduction? Before you can start to apply them, you'll need to shed

yourself of some all-too-familiar response reactions to certain familiar circumstances:

- The I-Thought-We-Were-Going-to-Share-Household-
  Chores response when one of you makes it clear that
  balancing checkbooks or cleaning ovens isn't going to
  be on *your* agenda!
- The I-Make-More-Money-So-I-Have-More-Rights response when professional and personal conflicts arise.
- The I-Have-to-Work-This-Out-Completely-on-My-Own
  response to job-related stress and decision-making. (A
  frequent variation of this is the You-Wouldn't-Under-
  stand-Anyway response.)
- The Children-(Or Other Partner)-Always-Come-First
  response when you or your spouse is faced with a
  golden, but risky, proposition.
- The Who's-Sorry-Now (also known as the Gloat) response when your advice isn't heeded.
- The If-You-Loved-Me-You-Would response when your
  spouse won't or can't help you with a major difficulty
  at work or at home.

All couples have been guilty of at least two of these
responses. They are ingrained into our marital culture. The
only way that we're going to change that culture is to
reshape those whining, guilt-glutted rejoinders into more
constructive phrases like:

I-Know-We-Both-Hate-to-Do-This-So-Let's-Take-Turns-or-Hire-Someone-to-Do-It-for-Us

This one is usually the easiest to change. When the task
is routine, take turns—with the proviso that no one will
blame the other for an occasional lapse. If the pinch-hitting
partner needs to learn how to perform the task, then the
adept partner should accept the role of temporary teacher
as part of the deal.

Consider delegating an outsider to take over at least

some of your odious chores. Help might be less costly than you fear. In many communities, dependable college students are available for housekeeping, bookkeeping, and other kinds of keeping at rates that are far lower than those of so-called "trained" professionals. Usually, the angst you save is worth the money. If you can't afford help for everything, pick out the most psychologically debilitating and start with that. As economics professors Freund and Kniesner put it, "There's no 'wife' in a two-career marriage. Both of you must learn to produce a wife from your relationship."

Let's-Think-About-How-This-Is-Going-to-Affect-Us-Both

Power Partners do not lord incomes or job status over each other. Just because you make more than your spouse doesn't mean that you get to decide on the family vacation or whether to put savings into stocks or CDs. Try and establish a teamwork attitude about any decision that might affect your partner.

Dr. Zussman says that this situation occurs most often when one partner, usually the woman, goes back to work or school after being a homemaker. "A wealthy suburban couple I treated had real problems dealing with her revitalized career efforts. The man made an impressive income and enjoyed supporting his family in style. His wife decided to go back to her teaching after their children started school. She was successful at her job, even though her salary was small compared with his. But she now expected her spouse to treat her as a careerist and take up his fair share of housekeeping duties. He resented this because he felt that his lion's share of earnings made his position more important."

She believes that younger couples will change this persistent attitude, but slowly. "Each couple has residues of the former generation. People deal with their ghosts in different ways and at different paces."

Jay and Rema Goldberg are an unusual couple who have

surmounted some of their traditional obstacles. Jay, one of New York's most celebrated lawyers (he represented Carl "Andy" Capasso in the Bess Myerson case; more recently he became Donald Trump's divorce counsel), has been married for thirty years to his wife, Rema. She is president of her own stress management firm, representing clients like IBM, Texaco, and Hitachi. Theirs is an unusual relationship even in today's more liberal legal circles; she picks his juries.

"We're still products of our generation," she explains. "Jay and I are from traditional Jewish families where the wife's main role was to run the household and raise the children. Even though I've always taken an active role in Jay's practice, it wasn't until the 1960s and the advent of feminism that I began to question the amount of time Jay spent helping out at home and with the kids. It's really the one area of friction in our relationship—I still have some regrets that he wasn't home that much when the children were little."

Jay also admits that if Rema were suddenly to become the major breadwinner in the family, it would trouble him. "I worry about people changing. I see this happening in my work. It would definitely cause problems if I wasn't making most of the money. We haven't as yet been tested on this point. I don't know how I would react."

Yet this dynamic pair is light-years ahead in other aspects of Power Partnering, as you will see further on in this chapter. And they have managed to hang in there despite some fundamental differences in their viewpoints.

Sometimes couples find themselves in professional circles that encourage these long-standing attitudes. This is especially true for female partners.

"I see this too much in the academic world," says Deborah Freund. "When I was in graduate school over ten years ago, a professor told me that he never gave women a higher grade than B-minus because they'd never end up pursuing a longtime career. Once, when Tom was getting an award at a major southern university, I mentioned that I couldn't attend a certain luncheon because I had a date with a former student. It became clear from the conversation that several faculty members thought my student had 'graduated' from kindergarten to grade school!"

Listen-I-Need-Your-Help-on-This

First off, it's flattering. You think highly enough of your husband's or wife's opinions to consider them desirable counsel. It's never a sign of weakness to ask for help from someone who really *can*. As you become better co-mentors, you'll get to know more about each other's workplace. But even without knowing many details, you should be able to start your spouse on an insightful path into his or her troubles. Just ask. And then listen . . . carefully! By providing a calm sounding board, you've already provided enormous doses of first aid.

As for playing the stiff-lipped martyr and sweating it out alone . . . why did you get married in the first place? Just as a whole generation of men are learning that it's okay to reach out, and even cry once in a while, professionally aggressive women are staging emotional lockouts in the name of feminism. Not sharing the load isn't feminist, or macho—it's dumb. Two heads *are* better. Start talking (and listening) to the one you live with.

Can-We-Afford-the-Risk-Right-Now? Or, Let's-Say-the-Worst-Happened

You get an offer to edit a new magazine, open a new store, or market a new gadget. The opportunity is exciting . . . and scary. No one likes to admit the possibility of defeat, so we use family stability as an excuse for not trying. If the project proves successful, you flail yourself for failing to act. Instead, you should let your partner know about the potential situation right away. If the two of you agree that the risk is too great, so be it! Next time around (and there will be one, no matter the urgency of the pitch) you both might be ready. Better still, turning down this particular chance could get your creative juices flowing in other career directions.

If you decide to go for it, now is the time to play out worst-case scenarios. Don't pretend that a potential loss of one income or a radical relocation won't affect your current lifestyle. Or your ability to take care of future emergencies. This is the time for a togetherness contingency plan. Although Robert and Barbara Taylor Bradford have earned international fame from her many best-selling novels and from his successful television mini-series, they retain a healthy attitude toward how fleeting fame may be. "If our fortunes suddenly changed," Barbara says, "we'd start all over again. We're both very ambitious."

Boy-Do-I-Ever-Feel-for-You

All right, sometimes a little internal gloating is good for the psyche. But it's never good for the soul of a co-mentoring marriage. If your spouse didn't listen up, he or she may have had a good reason. Besides, are your methods and strategies always infallible? Find out what went wrong and why. Don't chastise—ask questions instead. Now is the time to volunteer a back rub—not more advice.

All-Right-But-Give-Me-a-Good-Reason

You don't have to *like* the fact that your partner appears to be copping out—just express that disappointment in a direct manner. Maybe there's something about your request that could cause a conflict of interest for your partner. Love usually has nothing to do with situations like these, so don't escalate a small-scale letdown into a dramatic emotional infidelity.

However, as with any professional situation, you should exercise your right to know. If your partner refuses to discuss the matter at that moment, try bringing it up at a later, less tension-fraught time. Make your mate aware of *how* much his or her rebuff hurt. And if it didn't (be honest, now), don't play the dangerous game of pretending that it did. Let go and get on with solving the problem yourself. There are probably others around who'll be more willing to help. Turn toward them—not against your spouse.

These aren't the only response reaction changes you'll both have to work on. Other common less-than-powerful responses include:

- Only-Men (Or Women)-Should-Do-That
- Why-Can't-We-Be-More-Like-the-So-and-Sos?
- You-Promised-That-Would-Never-Happen-Again

You and your partner know which ones we're talking about.

Once you begin to free yourselves from stock responses, other areas of your communications system will also show marked improvement. These revamped response reactions can be carried over into your professional lives, too. A key element of Power Partnering is learning to adapt home smarts to workplace smarts . . . and vice-versa.

SEPARATION ANXIETY

Just as children frequently find it stressful to leave their parents' side on the first day of school, you and your partner may find it strange to separate your co-mentoring selves from the rest of your relationship. However initially awkward, this is a necessary step that will prevent the two of you from getting sidetracked. You'll never have time to promote each other's career goals if you don't lay down some ground rules. Here are some basic separation tactics:

1. Don't initiate a Power Partnering session when you want to focus attention on another aspect of your marriage. It's dishonest and unproductive to ask your spouse for tactical help with an uncooperative boss

when what you'd *really* like to know is why foreplay was so abrupt last night.

2. Never *demand* professional counseling from your spouse. You wouldn't enjoy mentoring someone at work who was always telling you that it was your duty to improve his or her performance. If the situation is urgent, let your partner know and set up a discussion time that's good for both of you. Advice given under fire is rarely reliable.

3. Try to hold some of your co-mentoring meetings away from home. If the two of you work in the same city (or the same firm), make breakfast or lunch breaks together a regular event. Unless both of you are after-six energizers, dinner isn't the occasion for heavy work discussions. At breakfast, you're far more alert and distanced from your respective desks; the lunch hour frequently stands as the dividing line between initiation and completion of work. If your spouse comes up with a winning suggestion over pizza, there's still time to put it into action.

   If possible, make room in the family budget for a short visit to a local hotel or conference center. Industrial parks and multi-use malls often have a business-oriented hotel or extended conference facility in the area. There's even the chance that you can book a small meeting room at reduced rates if you go during off-peak hours. Better yet, try one of the schools or colleges in your neighborhood. If your children attend, it may be fairly easy to gain access for short periods of time. Do make it clear that you will not be renting *Wanda Whips Wall Street* during your stay.

   Couples lucky enough to own a weekend retreat of their own should set aside regular weekends to take stock of their lives. John and Ellie Raynolds "hide" at their Vermont house at least two times per month. "We also 'black out' certain vacation periods for recharging our batteries," says Ellie. "You have to work at time allocation."

When one or both of you use your primary residence as a home office, set aside certain rooms or zones as serious work spaces. Even couples living and working in cramped apartments find it easier to divide professional from personal activities if both partners have designated corners in which to retreat when the business hat is on. Jewelry designer Angela Cummings usually works out of a tower office adjacent to their Connecticut home. Unpredictable musician and composer Frank Zappa and his wife, Gail, also run his audio/video enterprises from their California house.

Note: If you and your spouse work for the same company, it's *not* a good idea to meet in one of your offices with the door closed. Unless, of course, you *want* people to think that there's something sneaky going on. Your supervisor isn't going to imagine the two of you locked in a stolen embrace—she's going to assume that you're hatching plans for her early demise.

4. Dress the part. Wear businesslike attire if it helps to establish a professional atmosphere. Bring along the accoutrements of getting ahead. Take notes on legal pads or on your computer (many new software programs have "clipboard" or "memo" modes). Follow up the meeting with a quick note to yourselves about what took place.

5. Be polite. Many couples take good manners for granted. If you have to break a date, let your partner know so he or she can make other plans. *Thank* your spouse for his or her time and help. Here's where being married co-mentors can be more fun than the other kind; a department head might get mixed signals if you sent her flowers or bought him a pair of silk boxer shorts. Your Power Partner will get the right message!

NETWORKING BEGINS AT HOME

The 1980s saw a new generation of buzzwords emerging from the mouths of men and women who suddenly decided that Inner Peace could best be achieved through Upward Mobility. Bad Karma meant no Keogh plan, and the leveraged buyout became an intoxicating drug. Jerry Rubin, onetime hippie and political activist, began pushing a new philosophy of better living—*networking.*

The idea was that if you wanted to get ahead in your field, you should meet large numbers of like-minded people from all walks of professional life. By exchanging cards and following up with overpriced white wine and salads, you would gain inside-track information about your own situation. At first, the whole concept seemed fun and even bore fruit for those who didn't partake of too much Chardonnay. But eventually, inside tracking led to excesses of inside information and networking took on the connotations of greed and self-aggrandizement.

Today's successful Power Partners have learned how to make innovative use of networking by putting an intimate spin on its more calculating dimensions. "I get a double dose of pleasure and usually profit from putting my wife in touch with useful information and people," says Barry, a firm believer in this system. "Sheila's trying to put together a volume of celebrity fairy tales for a major publisher. I'm a sound engineer for an L.A. recording studio, so I've gotten pretty friendly over the years with some of the heavyweights. I can't say who right now, but one of the sexiest chart-toppers in town is sprucing up this totally romantic, innocent story she wrote in junior high school. My wife got a news-breaking contribution, and I got the chance to remind Ms. Platinum who cleaned up those fuzzy top notes on her last album."

Think of intramarital networking as a game. You start with two players: you and your spouse. The playing board is your combined work territories. Now envision the vast variety of individuals you see while moving around that great big board. The challenge of each round is one partner's specific networking need. The goal is to find the right person from anywhere on the board to help with the task at hand. Remember: the right person can also be a conduit to solving the problem by knowing other useful people who aren't on the board to begin with.

As you and your spouse begin to play, start making a written list of who's who among potential contacts. Each of you may learn some surprising information about your own, as well as your mate's, place of employment. Although the game board we have in mind is imaginary, it's not such a silly idea to draw some rough sketches of your real-life offices. Taking yourselves on a guided tour can be a real eye-opener.

"Colin and I actually did something like this on a snowy night when the cable box blew out," remembers Lisa, a staff pediatrician for a Denver hospital. "I had been trying to find someone to fund a new walk-in clinic for months, but with my line of doctoring, I don't meet too many graying philanthropists."

"Neither do I," says Colin, laughing. He manages the ski lift facilities at several major resorts in the Denver vicinity. "But then I realized how many wealthy, influential people my clients know. I asked Lisa to draw a picture of what the clinic would look like—how much space, how many beds, how much staff, all the stuff that someone who knows budgets can relate to. I took her doodlings and some more organized materials to the owner of one of the lodges I work with. This guy kind of owed me one because I taught his grandson to ski. Nothing's definite yet, but Lisa and her medical board have some promising meetings in the works."

Even couples in seemingly unrelated fields have discovered intriguing ways to cross their contact matrices. Marvin and Gertie Max are such an enterprising Kansas City couple. He's a bank president and she's an educational entrepreneur and former teacher. Gertie's sterling reputation as an educator helped her husband for years, and now his client list is helping to build international sales for her Study Systemizer Kit.

Play this game at a time when the two of you are relaxing together. Discovering useful contacts for getting ahead should not be dealt with as intensely as solving the problem of a back-stabbing co-worker, or facing the reality of an imminent takeover or strike. As with everything else in Power Partnering, there are some crucial boundaries of prudence and taste that should rarely, if ever, be crossed.

- Never discuss this kind of game-playing with ANY-ONE except your spouse! A careless remark to a co-worker at *any level* could spell disaster for one or both of you. Even your best friends should be kept in the dark. New York, Los Angeles, Chicago, and Miami can turn into Peyton Place Central faster than an inter-office fax.
- When you've picked out some potential networking helpers from the board, think carefully about possible danger zones of conflicting interests and indiscretion. Feel the situation out before you make a concrete move on your partner's behalf.
- In the same spirit as A, don't discuss the outcome of these dealings, whether or not they're successful. The helpful other will take care of his or her own publicity campaign; most bridge-builder types like to remain in the shadows. Naturally, an appropriate token of appreciation (even for trying) is always in good form. A dinner invitation, a modest gift . . . better yet, a similar favor in return should the time come.

BUDDY SYSTEMS

Each of you entered your relationship with a string of friends from all phases of your life. Many of them probably have developed interesting careers and abilities. Encourage your spouse to develop his or her own amicable bond with acquaintances who could prove useful networking allies.

Volunteering is always a great way to meet prominent community leaders. Join the local food or clothing drive . . . or start one yourself. Offer to talk with high school and college students who want to learn more about your profession. Even if your involvement is less than wholly altruistic, the end results will be beneficial to those around you as well as to yourselves.

Maddie, a Florida high school principal, wanted to introduce a journalism program into the curriculum. She had always enjoyed listening to the stories about "the ones that didn't get away" told by her husband's former college roommate, Bob, now an editor at a Miami paper. When the moment came to put her teaching plan together, she called upon Bob's expertise. "He saved me a ton of time. He even offered to set up a vacation internship program for my best students. The school board really gave me high marks—and a raise—for that!"

When you do get together with people you haven't seen for a while, being able to play instant catch-up with their activities can give you a distinct advantage. Make file cards on couples who aren't regularly in your social swim. That way, when you and your spouse get together with far-flung acquaintances, the two of you will be pretty much up-to-date. You'll also be able to focus quickly on any potential networking needs.

Such friends can usually be trusted far more readily since they already come with a sense of loyalty to your mate. Of course, we're not talking about potentially awkward alliances with former beaux or girlfriends, unless they're from the *extremely* distant past. It's also important to be sensitive to your spouse's feelings; don't let him or her think that you're trying to "steal" the friend. And watch out for developing cases of the flirts! With all of this in mind, your spouse's cavalcade of buddies could turn into one of your biggest networking boons.

CROSSOVER TALENT POOLS

Another potent source of personal networking is your own combined talent pool. There's a good chance that *your spouse's skills* can provide you with fresh approaches and insights into many of your professional dealings. In situations where one spouse is a manager and the other is a staff member, sharing perspectives on each other's roles and responsibilities can reduce workplace anger and stress.

Valerie Roberson Williams is a senior stylist for a top-ranking fabric company. She creates original woolen and woven materials for designers like Giorgio Armani. Her husband, Lloyd, is the CEO of New York's Uptown Chamber of Commerce. "Lloyd is used to being in charge, which also means shouldering a lot of burdens. He deals with local and national politicians constantly, as well as major companies who are interested in doing business in Harlem. By hearing about the down side of being on top of the hill, I've become a bit more sympathetic toward my own bosses."

In contrast, Lloyd has benefited from his wife's professional position. "Valerie allows people who are close to me to see me better. I have a hard veneer; she lets other sides of me come through. Through her, I've learned to relate better to my co-workers and associates. She's my strongest business asset."

Lauren and Michael Falk are always conscientious about using crossover skills to facilitate their individual businesses. "I handle all of Lauren's fashion newsletter's marketing and production work. This frees up a lot of her time. And she can trust me. In turn, I get briefings about style trends coming on the market. When Pepsico was bringing out Slice, they hired me to create a promotional tool. Lauren had gotten the beat on plastic watches before most of the country even knew what they were. I told my client to let us make one for the product. The whole concept was almost too new for them to accept, but eighteen months later, when they saw how popular those watches had become, Pepsico *really* listened when I gave them another winning suggestion. Lauren's savvy makes me look on the ball."

Partners should also encourage each other to increase their range of abilities. "Michael thought I should do more public speaking," says Lauren. "I was always timid, until he finally got me to take a course. Last spring, I ran my first seminar. The audience was really impressed, which gave me a huge confidence boost. Now I'm being considered to host a Detroit area radio fashion report."

"I organized and presented her slides," adds Michael with a smile.

Lauren and Michael have worked out a sensible personal code of ethics for these types of crossovers. "I never charge Lauren for my time, and since it's *our* bottom line, she knows that I'm going to get her the most competitive prices on materials and services."

"We're also sensitive to our clients' reactions at having a spouse 'brought in.' I was doing a piece on fashion in the U.S.S.R. at the same time that Michael was working on marketing projects for a major brand of Russian vodka. I wanted to do a tie-in with my newsletter, but then we both decided that the client might feel that we were being pushy. If one of us wants the other to back off, there's rarely any objection."

The Goldbergs have played the crossover game to its ultimate satisfying end with Jay utilizing his wife's psychological analysis talents. "It was a natural step for us," he remembers. "I had always practiced my summations with Rema. She knew all about my cases—I have always preferred to share work problems with my wife than with colleagues. I defer to her decisions regarding jurors."

"And even with judges," recalls Rema. "There was this one time when I told Jay that, in my opinion, the judge appeared to be an unusually fair man. I suggested that Jay dismiss the jury and let the judge decide the case alone."

"This is a very risky move, especially in federal cases," explains Jay. "Still, Rema's decision was once again the right one." And if he hadn't won the case? "I would never hold that against her, but, so far, it hasn't happened. Rema is so good at picking juries that she's doing it for other lawyers, too. She just got two acquittals for a colleague of mine." Ironically, there have been few objections to this courtroom teamsmanship. "Most lawyers and judges really respect Rema, and the jurors don't know that she's my wife."

Rema laughs. "During the Capasso trial, everyone thought that I was Andy's sister. That was one of the most exciting periods of our life. The people involved in that case were incredible. I juggled my schedule so that I could go to court every day. You can't imagine what it was like watching Sukhreet and her mother, Justice Hortense Gabel."

As you would with the Networking board game, spend a leisurely afternoon or evening going over each of your particular skills, strong points, and even areas that could use improvement. This is where psychologist Evelyn Sherburne's approach of defining a spouse's career through a series of linked abilities comes into play.

Write down what you think are your best and worst professional points. Have your spouse do the same. Then compare lists. Do you generally agree with each other, or are there vast differences of opinion? Explain your negatives and positives. Are you basing most of your answers on (a) what you hear from your spouse, (b) what you hear from those who work with your spouse, or (c) what you observe from your spouse's behavior when he or she is at home? Be sure to differentiate the three.

Next, start drawing lines from your column of positives to your partner's. Could your knack with spread sheets play an active role in helping your mate choose the right portfolio for demanding clients? Is your insight into labor relations going to give your spouse an edge in dealing with an irksome employee? Does your partner possess the patience of Job while you can't bear to deal with anyone who requires remedial training? By learning and "borrowing" from each other, you've already started to double your work efforts without adding much time or sweat.

Now see if some of your negatives can be balanced by your partner's positives. Is your tendency toward procrastination offset by your partner's impulse to plan ahead? Does his inability to delegate make him perfect for times when you'd rather not take total charge?

Mary and Richard, the hotel marketing director and real estate developer from the previous chapter, anticipate the day when they'll amass enough capital to start their own company.

"Mary and I complement each other so well," Richard explains. "I'm a broad-brushstroke kind of person—she actually enjoys sweating the details that drive me crazy."

See what you can *learn* from each other's inadequacies. At the very least, the two of you will find new ways to divide personal duties . . . by aptitude and attitude instead of gender and tradition.

HEADHUNTING

Executive search firms are booming. With companies and their employee pools expanding and contracting at incredible rates, it's easier and more efficient to hire an expert to find the best person for a particular position. You and your spouse can play this game, too.

Conduct "interviews" with each other. Take turns being the client, potential candidate, and the headhunter. This way, you both get to see *all three* perspectives. What are you looking for? What would your new boss require of you? How would the headhunter evaluate the match? Use this exercise in conjunction with other forms of personal networking. Before long, each of you will be more confident about (a) your own abilities, (b) your spouse's interest in helping you, (c) your potential for actually getting what you want.

"One rule we've worked out is never to let the other partner end up in a worse professional position," says Tom Kniesner. "There is an economic philosophy developed by John Rawls which can apply to professional couples: get the best job you can for the *weaker spouse*. Let that person rise to his or her maximum level of capability, even at the temporary expense of the other's career choice."

Adds his wife, Deborah, "Tom and I never even make a

follow-up call about a job nibble unless we discuss it first. So far, this system has paid off pretty well. But, then, we're equally confident about our levels of expertise and desirability as candidates. Not everyone is so secure about their professional worth."

THE ULTIMATE HUNTING GROUND

Why not right in your own backyard? You'd be surprised at how many couples have done this for each other (even though they rarely like to talk about it). A top editor at a major newspaper had a wife who had a high-level corporate position at a famous magazine. Her secret ambition was to helm that publication herself. When it looked as though that would never happen, her husband presented the situation to his own boss, who had just purchased a similar magazine for himself. Guess who ended up making that little-known monthly one of the publishing phenoms of the 1980s?

The wife has since gone on to perform the same editorial miracles for still another magazine, this time not owned by her husband's boss. Her husband has also moved on to other duties within his employer's realm. The point here is that without her spouse's high-stakes headhunt, she might never have gotten the chance to demonstrate her largely hidden and formidable editorial talents.

STAYING IN TOUCH

Just as a well-run company ticks along on a constant flow of information, a Power Partnership must consistently stay in touch with itself. Compare diaries at the beginning of each week (Sunday nights are a good time to organize the next six or seven days). Agree on time slots that you'll keep open for each other. Make sure that all social dates are coordinated, so you don't end up scheduling a round of squash the same evening as your partner's after-hours staff meeting. And don't be afraid to schedule in specific times for intimate interludes. There's nothing coldhearted about romantic planning. You can actually incorporate setting up sex in advance into your own fantasies. In that way, sex becomes a highly anticipated break in the routine.

"Planned sex is usually positive sex," Dr. Zussman agrees. "The buildup can bring you back to the heightened excitement of adolescence, where getting ready for a date was paramount in importance. Each of you can think about what you'll bring to your rendezvous—what you'll do to pleasure your partner and yourself—what you'll wear, what you'll do to enhance the mood—where you'll go before or afterwards." She doesn't think that incorporating some relaxed "shop talk" into lovemaking appointments is a bad idea, either, "as long as it's spontaneous and both partners are comfortable with the discussion."

Do try and keep outside disturbances to an absolute minimum. It's hard to control a crying baby, but incoming telephone calls can be picked up by machine. In those (we hope) rare instances where one of you absolutely, positively, must pick up that receiver, keep it short. The important rule here is to react as your partner would. "Of course Betty would pick up the phone if it was an urgent call, and so would I," says Boyd Matson. "We understand that about each other's jobs. We don't like it, but no one blames the other for interruptions."

Allow your spouse full access to all addresses, records, and files. Even if your personal finances are partially separate, the other partner should be able to have general information about, if not transaction rights to, all instruments. If one of you still has a "little black book," keep it in your office. But we assume that Power Partners have outgrown troublesome toys like that.

Let your partner know roughly where you'll be during the day. No one assumes that you're going to stick to a tight schedule, so don't worry if there are as many as a dozen changes in twelve hours. If one of you is going to a last-minute nighttime function or meeting, let the other know early enough (if possible) so that he or she can make some private plans for the evening. And if that occasion runs really late, do phone home. This is a matter of mental health and safety. And everyone needs a good-night kiss—even if it arrives via NYNEX or MCI.

SETTING GOALS

What is it that you both want to achieve? Where do you see yourselves in one year, five years, fifteen years? Still married, we trust, and a bit richer? Or maybe monetary security isn't the bull's-eye on the target. As we've said in our Introduction, your goals can be anything from an early retirement to the South of France to sending your kids to Harvard with hard cash. But, just as with conventional businesses, you have to set goals.

Otherwise you won't stick to your Power Partnering plans, and you'll find yourselves slipping back into your old marriage management patterns. These goals can start out small—saving up for an extended vacation or a summer rental. Or you might promise your spouse that you'll help her to leave her stagnating company by Labor Day. Your aims might be more organizational; the two of you may want to strive toward restructuring your personal lives to include more free time with family members, or even starting up a personal venture of your own.

Keep your sights fixed, but your timetables flexible. It's important to keep setbacks from discouraging committed perseverance. Remember, Power Partnering is as much an *attitude* as a working program of lifestyle improvement. If you and your spouse don't accomplish as much as you'd like in a given amount of time, don't waste more of the same agonizing over your presumed failure. This is *not* an "all or nothing" approach. Everyone hits the wall sooner or later. But those who learn to go around it usually reach the Emerald City while those who use it as an excuse to quit simply doze off in the poppy field and lose out.

BRAINSTORMING

When a marketing or advertising agency needs a new name for a product, they get a group of witty, quick-thinking cohorts into a comfortable room, and give them a general briefing. What follows is a rapid-fire, no-holds-barred creative rush of ideas for names. Nothing is rejected and both names and the mood get livelier and zanier. By the end of the hour, agency and client have a mile-long list of alternatives. Most will be unsuitable, but a golden short list will frequently emerge from the verbal chaff. The point is that harnessing *many* creative viewpoints in a tight time slot can sometimes prove more productive than working alone or even in pairs. While we continue to advise keeping most Power Partnering activities between yourselves, for some dilemmas, bringing in a select bunch of willing outsiders is the best solution.

Let's say one of you is starting up a company that makes organic baby food, as Diane Keaton did in *Baby Boom*. A catchy name and label are part of a successful marketing scheme. This is a case where calling in the troops will save time and energy. Don't limit yourself to potential consumers, either. A bachelor with a sense of humor might have the best ideas of all, because his frame of reference is so far removed from the product at hand.

You can call brainstorming sessions to order in your home (more about this in chapter 4), or at a more neutral location like the local Y or, if you're members, Rotary or other civic centers. Keep the mood light, upbeat, and informal. Food and nonalcoholic beverages are good incentives. Just make sure that your leadership skills are strong enough to keep the event from disintegrating into a gossipy party. This is still part of your problem-solving strategy.

WHY CAN'T A WOMAN BE MORE LIKE A MAN?

Professor Henry Higgins made his famous complaint in *My Fair Lady*. Too many executive men and women still wish that the other sex could get into their Jockey shorts or jogging bras for at least one day a year. Power Partners *actually can!*

By exchanging *gender information* about how men and

women approach and solve problems, each of you has a distinct edge on the competition. Like Lloyd and Valerie Williams, who give each other insight into management/subordinate dealings, couples who are sensitive and respectful of each other's gender differences can pick up on inside information of a different sort.

"Women *do* respond differently in some ways," says magazine consultant Lenore Hershey. Hershey, former editor in chief of the *Ladies' Home Journal*, feels that "women tend to be more analytical. They will stop and ask 'Why?' instead of plowing ahead. Men can move on more easily from situation to situation. They find it easier to adapt to what Henry James called 'the unattainable art of taking things as they come.'"

She also thinks that men tend to isolate themselves more and find it tougher to admit a mistake than most women do. "Even at the top levels of management, a woman doesn't like having that feeling of being alone in the big corner office. And she isn't as afraid of minor failures."

As two-career marriages become the social norm, these traits will begin to blend, possibly leading toward a new executive ethos that will benefit everyone. But, in the meantime, you and your mate can jump-start the process on a private level.

Go back and look at your individual strengths and weaknesses. Think about which ones *might* be more gender-linked. Present a current work problem to your spouse and see if he or she has a different approach based on a male/female point of view. This isn't an exercise in sexism—it's a discovery process into the subtle yin-yang that leads us away from the belief in single gender superiority. In business, as in marriage, some approaches are more effective than others. By expanding your reaction horizons, you will increase your repertoire of approach alternatives when your next professional decision comes up.

LEARNING TO DISAGREE

There will be times when you and your spouse won't see Partner-to-Partner on these and other strategies you will be developing for yourselves. A *fair* fight can clear the decks if you set up sensible parameters.

1. Confine your argument to the problem at hand. Don't let a disagreement over whether or not to ask your wife's boss for help on cutting through some of your occupational red tape turn into a ten-rounder over carpooling or in-laws.
2. If you find that the disagreement is escalating beyond its original importance, make a mutual decision to table the discussion until each of you has had more time to weigh your differences. Returning to the bargaining table with a calm emotional base can make a huge difference in outcome.

   Barbara Taylor Bradford comments, "I would listen to Bob if he offered criticism." But asked about Robert Bradford's television productions, she says, "I never interfere in the filmmaking because he knows better than I what will work. If an outside producer bought my book for filming, I wouldn't have any say. You *must* be able to separate the professional from the personal."

   Letitia Baldrige suggests offering comfort first. "Examine the situation. Try and find out what went wrong. You should make someone you love see the light."
3. Neither of you may have the skills you need to solve this dilemma effectively. Instead of wasting time, energy, and emotion, go out and find someone who has the knowledge to handle the crisis. The problem-solver could be a trusted friend or business colleague; it might even be one of your own children!
4. Don't lobby your spouse the minute he or she arrives home. Lynda Robb has learned the political art of holding that thought: "I keep politics out of pillow talk, even if it's something I feel strongly about. Chuck knows that he has a haven of peace when he walks through our front door. This doesn't mean that

I agree with everything he says or votes on—I just don't think that you should jump on a spouse when he or she is tired and vulnerable."

5. After finally coming to as satisfying an agreement as possible, do something relaxing and pleasurable together. Celebrate the fact that you *can* resolve these sorts of conflicts and not let it affect the rest of your relationship.

6. Make notes about the experience. The next time a disagreement arises, you can go back and see if what you went through before can save you angst this time around.

Show and Tell

You remember this one from grade school. Make it a regular part of your Power Partnering routine. *Show* your partner what you've been working on (unless it's absolutely confidential) that day. *Tell* your spouse about the negative and positive parts of your day. Don't forget to share the humorous moments. Most working couples actually find it relaxing rather than stressful to hear about the other half's triumphs and tribulations.

Brenda and Scott Burrows bring home entirely different scenarios and benefit from the different spheres of experience:

"Scott is full of talk about music industry intrigue, new arrangements, and upcoming gigs. While I know that his work can be as gritty as mine, it still has an air of show-biz excitement that lights me up. I give him a perspective on the nine-to-five world. I explain how corporate life works. He gets to see that his world's stuffed shirts aren't that different from mine."

This sharing has also helped each of them to hone their personal professional skills: "Scott's routine of always being on the prowl for new jobs has made me more aggressive about pushing harder for more responsibility at my PR firm. In turn, I've shown him some tricks about getting your foot in the door. Discussing our days is something we both look forward to a lot. Even if Scott gets home very late, I try and stay awake. He tries to be around the night before one of my big presentations, too. It's a luxurious feeling to have someone around who *wants* to know what you've been up to or what's coming up on tomorrow's agenda."

PARTNER ENVY

A surprising number of interviewees insisted that they never experienced this nasty but natural feeling. But if your career seems to be slumping while your spouse's is spiraling upward, jealousy and resentment over the other's good fortune are bound to surface. This can be especially true if both of you work for the same firm or share similar professional aspirations. It's hard to watch even a loved one collect first prizes while you're not even getting an occasional honorable mention. Don't turn into a Grimms' fairy tale villain. Remember, what's good for your *partner* is good for the *partnership*. While your spouse is on such a roll, ask yourself the following:

- How much of this winning streak is due to circumstances beyond either of your control? Sometimes we're dealt a royal flush simply because it's in the cards. No one *forced* millions of American teenagers to buy *Meet the Beatles.* No one preset America's TV dials to "The Cosby Show" or "Roseanne." The best reaction is to enjoy the ride while it lasts, and see what you can get out of it for yourself! Don't worry—things won't stay *that* good forever.
- Is your partner taking these good times in stride? Maybe your envy is stemming from your spouse's *reaction* to the circumstances rather than from the good fortune itself. This is not a time to allow communication to break down. Let your partner know that you feel left out. Chances are that he or she isn't fully aware of your jealous feelings.

• Are you bitter because *you* did not play a part in your spouse's success? You probably did without knowing it. Most partner support systems rely on steady supplies of encouragement and empathy rather than on pivotal acts of power. Maybe he or she simply hasn't defined your part in the proceedings enough for you to bask in the glow.

If you are the current occupant of the winner's circle, check out what's above to see if you've given enough credit to your partner for his or her contributions. And if you haven't looked down from cloud nine lately, remember that sooner or later you'll lose your catbird seat to someone else. Your spouse will still love you even when your professional stock starts falling.

OVERWORKERS NOT SO ANONYMOUS

There's been plenty written about the single and married workaholic. This is a condition that leads to burnout for the victim and those in his or her wake. More common, especially among two-career couples, is the unintentional overwork syndrome. Neither member of the marriage might start out as a compulsive worker, but, because of unanticipated responsibilities and assignments, one or both ends up with too much overtime. While the stress may not kill them, it can wreak havoc with their relationship.

"This kind of pressure creates problems with sex," says Dr. Zussman. "Fatigue sets in, and support breaks down in other parts of the marriage. Being tired becomes the excuse for everything." Zussman shows how the line of blame progresses. "The anger is first generated toward the spouse's office. The man or woman will start by blaming 'the boss' or 'the client' for long hours and too much work. But soon, the focus shifts to the partner.

"There's also the case where one spouse comes to enjoy work more than sex and other forms of spousal affection," she explains. "The libido becomes invested in the work instead of the partner. Men have always had this capacity, but more women are falling prey. These individuals get a genuine kind of sexual pleasure from professional success. It can be practically orgasmic. They turn less and less to their human sources for the same kind of feelings."

Overworkers tend to lose the ability to connect with each other even when they have the time. "We're at that stage where it takes so much effort to catch up with each other's lives that we just don't bother trying," says Wendy, a fast-track Chicago investment banker. "My husband's a surgeon. He's just as involved with work as I am. We both enjoy what we're doing, but sometimes I wonder what our relationship is about—what's the point of having someone to share your life with if you don't have time to get to know each other?"

Part of Power Partnering is learning to set your priorities up in favor of the *marriage* over the career. This doesn't always come naturally to couples with high professional drives. Just as Deborah Freund and Tom Kniesner won't pursue job leads that put the "follower" partner in jeopardy, you and your spouse should strive to create partnering ethics that prevent outside work from constantly intruding upon your marriage. Are you or your spouse suffering from this overwork syndrome? Think about what follows:

- Is sex becoming another routine obligation? Do you frequently find yourself thinking about work problems when you're making love? Do you and your partner find yourselves arguing more about sexual activity?
- Can you honestly remember the last time you and your spouse spent any length of time together in a non-work-related capacity? When was the last time you went to a movie, took a walk, or did some leisurely shopping together?
- Do you find yourself more irritable than usual with your children? Are you up-to-date about their progress at school and other activities? Are they less affection-

ate with you or your spouse? When was the last time
you went one-on-one with each child?

- How long has it been since you've gabbed with your
best friend? Is it getting harder for you and your
spouse to see people socially on a casual basis? Does
getting together for a relaxed spur-of-the-moment
meal mean a major production?

- If asked, can you talk about the latest important world
events with some degree of accuracy and interest? Are
you fairly current on what's going on around you?

- When did you last get out that needlepoint or those
oil paints? Have you gotten around to refinishing that
antique cabinet the two of you bought last spring?
When was the last time you and your mate attended
religious services or took part in other introspective
activities together?

Overworkers, unlike true workaholics, aren't necessarily
living for or through their professional loads. They are often
aware that life is becoming unbalanced, but feel helpless
about correcting the problem. Power Partners who've made
it across this potentially deadly chasm have learned the
value of many suggestions we've made in this chapter, such
as making time for each other. Such as turning to each other
first instead of last. Such as becoming better acquainted
with each other's on-the-job responsibilities.

LETTING GO OF THE PAST

One of the hardest lessons for any couple is learning
when to let go and move on. This is essential for Power
Partners because they are always running the risk of offering
help and advice that might not pan out.

This can cut two ways. If your professional and personal
lives are going well, it can be an ego-bolstering exercise to
look back and see how far you've come. But if one or both of
you has hit a temporary slump, tinkering with the time

machine can cause bitterness. Each of you must accept that change will be the *single constant*.

As Paul McCartney has remarked about his career, "You can't be peaking all the time. It slightly offends me that people ask why I keep on doing it. What I do is sing and write songs." Just as Paul's coming to terms with his past has finally allowed him to feel comfortable enough to perform Beatles compositions along with his solo materials, so all success-oriented people must accept that the stock ticker will continually rise and fall. That's no excuse to stop working, or give up on goals.

The past should become a cozy, inviting attic where you and your spouse can retreat for some forgotten advice or a deserved round of distant applause. There's nothing wrong with enjoying the occasional rainy afternoon thinking about the time you underbid that industry giant and got the contract. Or momentarily reliving the night you won an Emmy Award. Constructive reminiscing can help you resolve current and future problems. Cheerful attics filled with past victories are positive places to visit, far better than gloomy, cobwebbed cellars of failure. Just don't linger too long.

ENJOY YOUR ADVANTAGES

Question: When is it a great idea to sleep with your mentor? The answer is more obvious than black satin sheets. In her recent book about office romances, Lisa A. Mainiero, Ph.D., writes about how men and women on their way up should never indulge in sex with a professional mentor. You lucky devils! Not only *isn't* this one of your no-nos, but a lusty love life happens to be one of your most vital Power Partnering tools. You should never stop thinking of your spouse in sexual terms, even when he or she is editing your presentation or teaching you how to argue with your boss. Keep the fires under control until you shut down shop . . . but keep them burning.

Another distinct advantage enjoyed by couple co-mentors is reduced fallout from risk. Everything we've suggested in this chapter is risky to some degree. But you have the choice of moving at your own pace. If your work mentor is someone who also pays your salary and expects you to perform perfectly at 8:30 A.M. 350 days of the year, saying "not ready" isn't that simple.

Power Partners give each other breathing space and learning time. Mistakes won't send you back to the mailroom. Most office mentors are too busy worrying about their own bottoms and bottom lines to go to bat for you in a real crunch—especially if you rise too swiftly for their political comfort.

Have you ever given advice to a bright, less experienced friend or colleague, only to discover that he or she used your handy tips to sell you out? When Michael Jackson got friendly with Paul McCartney, he wanted suggestions about how to invest his newly minted millions. The elder statesman rock millionaire advised him to buy up lucrative music publishing copyrights . . . as Paul had done with rights to songs of Buddy Holly and to Broadway hits like *A Chorus Line* and *Annie*. Later, when the bulk of the classic Beatles catalog went on the block, Jackson outbid Paul and gobbled up the song rights for himself.

Or perhaps you've experienced the type of boss portrayed by Sigourney Weaver in *Working Girl*, who pretends to dish out advice (usually wrong) in order to mine her trainee's fresh lode of ideas. But Power Partners don't play these games with each other. All wins are team victories, so it doesn't matter if the goal was scored by the student or the teacher.

Deborah Freund remembers how her husband, Tom, showed her the ropes when he was a successful, tenured professor and she was just starting out at the same university.

"I hadn't really gotten a mentor for myself in graduate school," recounts Deborah. "Tom showed me how some of my work priorities were out of synch with what academia required. Up until then, I had been working for a large health care concern—an entirely different world from publishing papers and teaching. He would urge me to write more, to spend time with the right people. I was slightly jealous because I saw Tom going to these cocktail parties to which *I* wasn't invited. He would tell me that I shouldn't feel discouraged, but be patient. That was how the social scene worked on campus. You had to put in your time and pay your dues. I had jumped to the wrong conclusion that I was being snubbed. Tom was right. Several years later, I was on the party list, too. His coaching was extremely critical, and it's paid off for both of us." Deborah could trust Tom and his mentoring strategies because he *wanted* his wife to win.

Lynda Robb says she always thinks of her husband Chuck's campaigns in terms of "We won" or "We didn't make it this time." No matter how secure and positive the relationship, no office mentor can offer quite the same kind of tangible and emotional boosts, because there's always the danger that the protégée will end up taking over.

You've now seen the vast benefits of Power Partnership and how to go about getting them. You and your spouse have commenced your home networking efforts, you've begun to reestablish your joint goals, and agreed to rid yourselves of roadblocking responses that stand in your way. The next three chapters show you how to use these new skills and commitments to your best advantage.

Today's business court is so fast that even the Dreyfus lion and the Merrill Lynch bull can trip up. Power Partners are match-tough. It's not easy to beat down an unswerving alliance of uncompromising love and determination. But why worry about beating them when you can join them on the winning side of the net?

3

SYNCHRONIZED FISHBOWL SWIMMING

♦

Once you master Power Partner techniques, your achievement potential will accelerate—perhaps more rapidly than anticipated. Without time to adapt, you and your spouse may be thrown into a sea of unexpected pressures that come from your sudden visibility. All at once, colleagues and company heads expect you to offer decisive opinions before audiences. Total strangers scrutinize your appearance and that of your spouse. You're ambushed by reporters bearing questions you'd never ask your worst enemy. There are rounds of hands to shake, parties to attend, and business meetings to breeze or muddle through.

Today's careerists may face these challenges without necessarily becoming household names. In today's fiercely competitive environment, ambitious lawyers, university economists, and advertising executives must endure the scrutiny of their peers if they are to advance in their fields. And they must do this without upsetting the precarious equilibrium of the marriage, so easily shattered by slights to the ego. Without preparation, even a strong marriage can be eroded by jealousy or an unbalanced support system. The pressures of public speaking or "working" a room were daunting enough in the days when traditionally one spouse—the husband—was the undisputed achiever. They are intensified enormously when *both* partners are renowned in their respective businesses, and possessed of equal determination to succeed.

Marriages between celebrities of equal fame are notorious for being short-lived. That's understandable; when a husband and wife are both public figures, the strain of life in the fishbowl is magnified. The corrosive effect of career jealousy and bottom-line one-upsmanship usually precedes infidelity. Instead of being Power Partners, spouses become sparring partners—and, inevitably, jockeying for position in the professional arena spills over into the bedroom.

Supersuccessful celebrity couples whose marriages nonetheless appear unshakable personify Power Partnering at its most sophisticated. Their "solid as a rock" unions are a lesson in how to handle the stress of the celebrity whirl—whether "celebrity" means the cover of *People* magazine, or the quieter pressure of renown in a specialized business.

Recording artists Ashford & Simpson, best-selling novelist Barbara Taylor Bradford, fashion designer Donna Karan, Congresswoman Pat Schroeder, TV faces Judy Licht, Boyd Matson, and Barbara Walters, along with everyone else who's ever had a microphone shoved under their nose or struggled to stay awake during a six-hour awards ceremony, aren't that different from the rest of us.

The renowned reap the same Pyrrhic victories that bring monetary gains or global status at the cost of sleepless nights and sheer exhaustion. Some of these recognized couples and individuals have larger paychecks and perks—they also have bigger headaches and rougher responsibilities.

Lucky ones have learned how to make the most of their public moments by relying on dedicated partners to pull them through—no matter what.

Congresswoman Pat Schroeder and her husband, Jim, a prominent attorney, admit that her brief but significant run for the presidency didn't affect either of them very much because they had gotten used to being scrutinized and quoted.

"It was different for us than for Geraldine Ferraro and her husband," says Pat. "She never had that kind of intense public examination before. New York has so many more representatives than Colorado. In my state, each of us is constantly being watched and challenged. For example, we're used to making our taxes a matter of public record."

Her husband is equally matter-of-fact about public attention. "If you're thrown into something stressful without adjustment time, it can be very hard," he acknowledges. "But the media are part of our system. You just have to accept that."

The Schroeders have never brought their children along on the handshake circuit. "That's really kept the peace," Pat admits. "I see some of these other political families where the kids are rushed out of bed on Sunday mornings, dressed up like bandboxes and paraded around county fairs and other events. My children wouldn't have stood for that."

Ashford & Simpson, a couple whose relationship is as strong and uplifting as their music, have been able to put global acclaim into proper perspective. Valerie Simpson explains, "As songwriters, we got our start backstage. Nick and I saw what can happen when you hit the lights. Because there are two of us, we're better grounded. If one of us gets carried away, the other can say, 'Darling, come on!' We don't take stardom so seriously—it's more like having a bigger job with more benefits and responsibility."

Nick Ashford agrees. "Life became more fun when we became famous. I love giving to an audience. Recognition made us feel like kids starting out on a new road. I don't feel bad about our children growing up in a celebrity family. I think that you're born to it, like royalty. You have certain obligations, but there are also many wonderful opportunities."

Even when her feet were bleeding, Ginger Rogers was able to dance for the camera because Fred Astaire always made her look good; his ego strength permitted him to offer *more* than enough support. This usually unflagging professional generosity served him as well as his incomparable talent; to this day, it's difficult to find anyone disloyal to his memory.

Confident co-mentors should practice the same magnanimous steps. Women who are thrust into the leading position can learn how to keep from crushing a male partner's pride (and feet) while gliding across the ballroom floor. Men accustomed to setting the pace need to adjust their internal rhythms when asked to rhumba instead of foxtrot by a dynamic mate on the move. Those who give balance and support seldom stumble—even when the music gets too loud and the room temperature soars.

The reward for working on your public self-presentation is recognition without emotional wreckage. Don't worry about the flotsam and jetsam, or the unpredictable tide of public sentiment. British actor Michael Caine once said that his mother's motto was: "Be like a duck: calm on the surface, paddling like hell underneath." By synchronizing your social strokes, you'll soon progress from hard paddling to a graceful glide, while the rest of the world treads water.

THE FAME FACTOR

Andy Warhol's statement that "everyone will be famous for fifteen minutes" has become a reality. Fame doesn't always mean being asked for autographs or having your face on the cover of *People*. Become successful at whatever you do, and chances are you'll receive public recognition for your efforts. You may be celebrated in your hometown or within your professional circle. An unanticipated gesture or strong public opinion can position you on page one as swiftly as a hit movie.

Changing careers can move you from modest levels of visibility to worldwide eminence or notoriety. Ronald Reagan was no Clark Gable, but as a politician, he became more famous than a five-time Oscar winner. Tracey Ullman's records barely rippled the U.S. charts, but as an actress, she's become one of this country's hottest TV properties. These are both examples of famous people who had the self-inclination to change gears, and the right spouses to support them in their intuitively correct decisions.

It may not be you but your spouse who turns on the unexpected spotlight. Real estate man John Zaccaro was, no doubt, proud of the fact that his wife was the first female candidate for U.S. vice president—until he discovered how much public prying this honor entailed. A doctor or lawyer can be both successful and invisible, but what if the doctor achieves a major medical breakthrough or the lawyer wins a controversial case? Your spouse is an inventor, or a writer, or a chef. For years, the two of you work to keep his or her dream alive. But if and when the dream becomes reality, you face a new set of potential problems.

Most of us associate fame with wealth and privilege. While those desirable accompaniments can come with the package, so do not-so-delightful extras like invasion of privacy, added performance stress, intramarital competition, and, in extreme cases, loss of identity. You run the risk of being misquoted in everything from supermarket tabloids to the nation's most respected daily newspapers. For while fame persists, your personal life is no longer wholly your own. The more high-flying the fame, the harsher the criticism . . . and the harder the fall. As Lynda Robb puts it, "When you reach the top of the mountain, there's always someone waiting to throw rocks."

Power Partnering skills will help both of you achieve success and the fame that may well come with it. They will also allow you to enjoy your glory days and stave off the damage to your relationship that can occur with public acknowledgment. Couples who have learned how to support and balance each other usually cope better with life on the front line and front page.

SHARING THE DREAM

It's no accident that Barbara Taylor Bradford's famous trilogy of a successful, self-made woman and her family should bear the respective titles: *A Woman of Substance*, *Hold the Dream*, and *To Be the Best*. Those are the goals of most ambitious people. Barbara's fictitious heroine, Emma Harte, makes her fortune and finds worldwide recognition, but, in the end, she can't achieve true contentment until she finds a partner who shares her vision and isn't threatened by her drive or fame. The author's inspiration comes from her own marriage.

"Bob always knew that I wanted to be a novelist," she says. "The best thing he ever did for my career was to marry me! He wasn't afraid of my potential success because he was secure about his own business expertise. Besides, *A Woman of Substance* didn't exactly take off overnight. It wasn't until the book came out in paperback that it started to break sales records. We both had time to adjust. Bob, being a Hollywood producer, knew what 'going public' meant; my journalist background also prepared me for what might happen."

Adds Bob, "I'm not insecure. If they want to call me Mr. Taylor Bradford, that's okay—I'm very proud of Barbara." Barbara's latest novel, *The Women in His Life*, focuses on a highly successful man and the bevy of strong women who surround him.

Advertising legend Jerry Della Femina feels the same way. "In fact," he admits, "I always make our restaurant reservations under my wife's name. We get much better treatment when they know that Fox Television's Judy Licht is showing up for dinner. Of course, when we go to an *Italian* place, my name has more clout."

Other couples such as Avon's VP and director of corporate communications, Gail Blanke, and her husband, Jim Cusick, a former CBS news director who now runs his own video communications company, are lucky because they have different attitudes about being up front instead of backstage.

"I'm a show person," admits Gail. "I like the limelight— that's where the thrill is for me. Jim's thrills come from backstage victories. We take great pleasure in each other's wins and recognition. I think that's because we didn't marry each other for success. When we started out, neither of us ever dreamed that we would have come this far. I know that I fell in love with Jim's potential and his values. Jim was far more famous than I was when we were first married, and I loved that, too. Competition has never been a problem for us."

Adds Jim, "Gail's more of the ham—I'm kind of shy. We complement each other very well. That's why we can cheer each other on when one of us takes a giant step. Gail's always been extremely secure of her own professional identity; she's the one who's made me reach outside myself and take more risks."

Nor does it appear to be a marital difficulty for Barbara Walters and her second husband, entertainment mogul Merv Adelson. "It was important that I married a man who was successful and independent on his own," she says. Walters matter-of-factly adds, "He knew what he was marrying. He led a low-key life until we got married. He's still that way. He wouldn't discuss me if you called him for an interview; I try not to answer questions about him."

Dr. Zussman believes that when one partner becomes recognized, there is a danger that the "invisible" mate feels like a second-class citizen. "Sometimes the sought-after spouse comes to prefer the public adulation more than his or her partner's affection. Narcissism sets in."

Or as a famous dancer puts it, "You begin to believe in your own press clippings."

Actress Kathleen Turner readily admitted in a Barbara Walters TV interview that she would hate being married to another member of her profession. "It would always be 'You made three movies this year, and I only made two.' Actors are also the vainest people in the world." She is currently married to businessman Jay Weiss. Turner also affirms that she's sometimes happier being "Mrs. Weiss."

"It's easier when I'm away from home on a set. There's more respect. I've also been concerned that I'm too aware of my public role as Kathleen Turner."

It's important for the other partner not to feel unwanted

and insignificant. Spouses should work toward bolstering each other's worth and sense of self. Lynda Robb recalls how a female friend worried constantly about anything happening to her politician husband lest she lose her identity as his wife. "She finally went out and got a career of her own," explains Lynda. "It's hard for people who live close to the limelight. No one wants to be 'the wife of' anymore. That's true for any career, not just politics or show business. It helps that Chuck and I think of his political career as something *we* do together."

Letitia Baldrige, herself married to a powerful and highly private real estate developer, Robert Hollensteiner, thinks that the female spouse at the center of attention must be extra tactful and enthusiastic about her husband's public and private worth. "Women executives should push their husbands to the fore. Use their correct names, and don't forget to tell those around you what *they* do for a living."

Fredrica Friedman, vice president, executive editor, and associate publisher at Little, Brown & Company, has made numerous literary deals with well-known individuals. "I once attended a dinner party," she recalls, "where there was an extremely famous couple who made the rest of us feel uncomfortable. The woman was so enamored of her own celebrity—the husband's role was simply as an ornament. It became painfully clear that his success meant nothing more than another sign of her importance."

A man, on the other hand, should never make "innocent" remarks about "the power behind the throne," or belittle his professional and marital partner with anecdotes that place her in stereotyped domestic roles. Or, even worse, tell stories that make her appear to look weak or incompetent.

Sometimes it's the female half of the partnership who must deal with the public aspect of this awkward situation. Marilyn Quayle is still annoyed with the media's obsession about her "control" over the vice president. "Of course you discuss things," she recently admitted to the *New York Daily*

News. "That's what makes a good marriage. I seek advice from Dan all the time on what I'm doing."

When asked for the hundredth time about being "the power behind the throne," Quayle gave the *News* reporter this snappy retort: "I think it's rather humorous. And I also think it's actually very insulting. If I were all that wonderful and powerful and had all of that extraordinary ability . . . first of all, I wouldn't have gotten married, wouldn't have made the choices we made. It's like saying I couldn't have done it on my own—that's very insulting—or that what I've done in my marriage is a mistake, which is also very insulting. My choices are not acceptable? That's insulting, too. I think I've made a very good life."

CHANGING PUBLIC PERCEPTIONS FOR THE BETTER

When asked for the perfect example of a couple who knows the value of mutual public support, Letitia Baldrige made this pronouncement: "Joan Ganz Cooney and Pete Peterson. They make each other shine." Others agree that the driving force behind "Sesame Street" and the former secretary of commerce are a definite plus on anyone's party list. While each is highly respected on his or her own merits, they work better together as a social team.

A close friend of the couple's once remarked that "Pete can be a very remote figure, a starchy personality, but she has opened parts in him that were closed off. Joan humanizes him."

Peterson relishes his wife's accomplishments. "She is a true senior partner, not a quote unquote wife or a junior partner," he said.

During the Reagan administration, no one hesitated to make fun of the president or Nancy as separate individuals. But how many times did you hear stand-up routines about their devotion as a couple? Their obviously genuine love and respect for each other provided a protective shield against even the toughest criticism and biting satire. Today, Barbara Bush is helping her presidental mate look more human simply by being herself. Because George is obviously devoted to Barbara, a woman who cares more about children's literacy than new fashion lines, his image as a family man is firm.

In the oft-perceived cold-blooded world of business, wives like Saul Steinberg's Gayfryd can warm up an icy image. Steinberg, the chairman of Reliance Group Holdings, has been taught the importance of becoming involved in cultural and sometimes controversial good works. Gayfryd's enthusiasm for the fine arts and PEN, the international writers' society, has rubbed off on her husband in the form of major donations. While this sort of spousal apple polishing appears more skin deep than sincere, it still has its place in the public psyche. And the public benefits from generous donations and gifts.

THERE'S A RUMOR . . .

Oprah Winfrey doesn't mind sharing the tabloid rumors about her private life with studio audiences. By inviting the public to share her disbelief and annoyance over stories involving her longtime beau, her diminishing weight, and her increasing wealth, she puts those fabrications in their nonsensical place. Successful couples can find gossip, rumors, and criticism doubly trying because of their united front. Double-whammy brickbats can hit home hard.

Tony Award-winning actress Joanna Gleason and her husband, Michael Bennehum, who heads up the Beagle Group production company, are often reluctant to give interviews about their personal lives, even though they are still far from being household names. In sharp contrast, Paul Newman and Joanne Woodward, now heading toward their thirty-fifth anniversary, once took out a $2,000 ad in the *Los Angeles Times* to prove that they were not coming a cropper, despite Paul's bouts with the bottle and problems with his son, Scott.

Even experienced fishbowl swimmers like Lynda Robb have trouble ignoring unflattering innuendos. She still smarts from last year's *Washington Post* magazine's less than complimentary portrayal of her and her family. "I get angrier when they say or imply negatives about Chuck or the girls than I do when they come after me," she says. "That particular piece actually made me look pretty strong, but at Chuck's expense. That's one of the media's favorite gambits—building up one spouse by tearing the other one down. Chuck has a thicker skin. He'll tell me that most people will just look at the picture. I'm much more sensitive. I remember once there was this photograph of Chuck with 'an unidentified blonde.' I should have just laughed it off, since the 'blonde' in question was our daughter! But I took offense at what the caption was implying. My family is extremely understanding, but even after all this time, it continues to bother me more than it should."

Actress Hattie Winston and composer/arranger Harold Wheeler have also dealt with the potentially destructive "rumor mill" syndrome that haunts so many entertainers and politicians.

Harold remembers one particularly unsavory incident. "We got a call from a friend in Connecticut who had been to a dinner party where the main topic of conversation had been our impending divorce; Hattie was leaving because I beat her."

"Naturally, we knew this was a ridiculous lie," says Hattie. "But you worry about how these things get started and how to stop them before there's more pain. I've even received anonymous notes hinting at Harold's infidelity. Maybe these people are envious of our life together. I just don't know."

What this couple has learned is how to release their fears and tensions by talking out their distress and anger. "Communicating our feelings is the only way," emphasizes Hattie. "Even when Harold and I bicker over standard family matters like who's overslept or missed a turn taking our daughter to school, we try and apologize to each other promptly. I know that I can't function being in a sour mood all day. Staying sensitive is the key. And that goes for helping a partner or child deal with your fame, too."

ANYTHING YOU CAN DO . . .

Confident co-mentors should be imbued with competitive spirit—but never against each other! Nothing looks weaker (or sillier) than a couple who uses a public occasion to display their personal games of one-upsman (or woman)ship. Wilma Jordan, president and CEO of her own investment firm, is married to George Green, president of Hearst Publishing International. Although fiercely aggressive with business competitors, the pair strives to maintain professional public togetherness.

Wilma recalls with mild horror an incident involving another business couple. "Around six or eight of us were to spend a long evening together for business and social reasons. George and I are used to these sorts of events, and usually find them reasonably pleasant and useful. But this one couple—quite well known in New York circles—began a verbal barrage that commenced over drinks and got worse as the night wore on. She would tell him that she knew more than he did about his work. Then he would make fun of her business suggestions. She would criticize the way he pronounced pecan pie; he would retaliate by telling her to fix her makeup. When it came time to go for after-dinner drinks, most of us were trying to figure out how to kick this duo out of our limo."

An even uglier story involves the heir apparent to a major energy company. This fortunate gentleman was certain to helm his firm after the current CEO retired at the end of the year. At the annual Christmas dinner dance, Mr. Lucky was the name on everyone's lips. One of the vice presidents thought that it would be a flattering gesture if he cut in on the "golden boy" and his charming, always delightful wife. Just as he softly tapped her shoulder, she threw her husband across the floor, grabbed the bewildered VP, and shouted, "Thank goodness someone finally rescued me! I've been propping up that SOB for thirty years—it's my turn for some fun!"

OBLIGATIONS: YOURS, MINE, OR OURS?

"If I have to look at one more piece of rubber chicken, I'll scream!" Even if the bill of fare is duck breast with honey and peppercorn sauce, the sentiments remain the same. Endless ballrooms filled with frozen desserts and faces. The most honored of guests has been known to succumb to a quick bout of dais doze. As one notable put it, "I'd rather have a nice fat check than a tedious dinner and another engraved blunt instrument for my desk."

Power Partners have learned to take these occasions in stride. More importantly, they've learned how to use corporate gatherings to their own advantage. They've also learned how to say *no*—to an event chairperson and to *each other*.

"When the spouse comes along, he or she should be enthusiastic or stay home," says Letitia Baldrige. "A supportive mate should be willing to mix. They should also make themselves aware of current affairs, innocuous company business matters, and other topics which are likely to surface during the event. Dumb wives and husbands are the ones who don't keep up."

"Chuck is a great social asset to me," says Lynda Robb. "I like having his company—he reinforces my commitment, and I do the same at his functions. Sometimes you go because it's good for one or both of you, and sometimes misery loves company. You keep smiling and hope that you'll meet someone worthwhile."

She also admits that there are times when spouses should let each other off the hook . . . or say "No thank you" in unison. "Chuck and I have worked out a system of honesty where if one of us would rather catch a movie or stay home with the girls, we ask each other if going along is *really important*. There have been many times when Chuck or I have gone through a less than terrific evening when it wasn't that vital to the other. There are times when it's better to act as an individual."

Judy Licht and Jerry Della Femina have two young children, heavy work loads, and tight time frames. "We've established priorities for ourselves. Jerry and I want to have at least three nights a week at home with the kids while they're so young. What we've learned to do—especially if the occasion is for business or charity—is to ask if our presence is truly needed. Most of our friends understand."

Then there's the question of how the "spouse" partner should conduct himself or herself during the event. In some cases, the mate who's not at the center of attention enjoys, as Judy Licht describes, "basking in the other's glow." At other times, the shadow spouse feels unwanted and out of place.

Marion Blakey is director of public affairs for the U.S. Department of Commerce. She formerly served as President Reagan's deputy assistant for public affairs. Blakey is married to Dr. William Dooley, an emergency care physician on staff at a Washington, D.C., area hospital. Each has strong feelings, positive and negative, about attending the other's endless stream of galas and meetings.

"I generally can't tolerate the 'spouse program' bit," admits Blakey. "Many of the doctors have nonworking wives. Fortunately, Bill is sensitive to my feelings, so I don't have to go unless it's my decision."

Dr. Dooley, on the other hand, usually enjoys his wife's top-drawer political social swim. "I'm more interested in what Marion does than she is in my world. That's just the way we are. I have to admit that going to the White House is exciting, and I'm a plus at parties because once all those jockeying politicians find out that I'm a doctor, they relax. They know that I'm not trying to get their jobs."

Adds Blakey, "When you're working at the White House, you feel that you should go to everything. Now that we have a baby, we try to stay home a bit more. But it's great that Bill likes Washington's social scene—this can be a tough town."

Blakey and Dooley move in such different circles that there's rarely any feeling of social competition or neglect. When it comes to doing the party circuit, they are secure enough about their marital partnership to permit each other to follow his or her own inclinations.

Other couples, like Licht and Della Femina, have, as many columnists observe, become self-admitted "masters of the walk-through," getting in and out of numerous parties in record time.

But what if you and your spouse aren't that secure, or aren't renowned enough to grab a mini-quiche, smile for the cameras, pose with the big shots, and run? What if staying all night, lending support to your department head or committee chairperson, is a critical part of the success agenda?

You can make it easier on yourselves and each other. Try and think about how to make yourselves shine, and whom you might meet. An investment banker at a dentists' society luncheon—what could be duller! But dentists make lots of money and are usually thrilled about meeting financial fast-trackers, so by introducing yourself, you've broken a multitude of conversation barriers. Dentists, like doctors, are daring and aggressive investors. Here's a chance to do a little business, perhaps? Or you might use small talk time to find out where dentists prefer putting *their* money. If the professional talk turns to innovative procedures or drugs, you might get an invaluable beat on where some of your own clients' cash might belong.

Smaller gatherings can be more stressful for the "odd spouse out." Again, it's up to the inside partner to help smooth the social path. Fredrica Friedman's husband, Stephen, is executive vice president and general counsel for the Equitable Life Assurance Society of America, and former commissioner to the national Securities and Exchange Commission. Yet even someone as prominent as Stephen can feel momentarily left out of the action in his wife's world.

"Fredi and I were at a party Charles Bronson gave for his wife, Jill Ireland. She had just published her book. The place was filled with Hollywood familiars who had little in common with me and my work. Even though she was busy making her rounds, Fredi found time to introduce me to someone she *knew* I would be delighted to meet—Steve Krantz, novelist Judith Krantz's producer husband. Like me, he's a businessman who is often placed in the same social position. We had a lot in common."

WHOSE FEELINGS COME FIRST?

A female restaurant owner recalls a pair of distinctive couples who came to dine and deal. "The two men were thoroughly engrossed in their merger negotiations. One of the wives suddenly pitched forward into her dish of linguine. She had obviously had one too many. Neither man missed a bite or business angle. The other wife just sat there, hesitating over whether to say something or keep working on her veal chop. She finally went to the ladies' room . . . for twenty minutes. By the time she returned, the men had finished their meal and discussion. I felt terrible for that woman."

Cringing at the sight of a put-upon spouse, male or female, is understandable. But Ms. Powder Room, as she shared later, was not as perturbed as one might expect; she was performing one of a Power Partner's toughest roles.

What the restaurant owner didn't see or hear was the private dialogue to come. When the pair was finally alone, his first words were "You were magnificent! I couldn't believe those two. Remind me to tell our CEO to keep her away from the barbecue pit at the next company outing." The wife knew, being a professional herself, that in a case like this, business takes precedence over personal comfort. This dinner wasn't about food, service, or conviviality—it was about merging two companies.

As they strolled into a posh hotel for a deserved nightcap, she remarked drily, "I guess the next time we book a table, we'd better use my name."

There are times to draw the line . . . or lead it in another direction. Most savvy corporations eschew business and social settings that could possibly prove insulting to a particular group or individual because of race, sex, or religious affiliation. Unfortunately, these clubs and associations still crop up in occupational entertaining. If your wife is an ardent feminist and you are both invited to dine with a client at his male-only membership establishment, straighten out your mutual feelings and strategies in advance.

Most secure professional women believe that their spouses do not subscribe to this type of segregation and, for the sake of the bottom line, will attempt to smile politely as they enter the lone "ladies permitted" dining room.

However, if the meeting place poses restrictions that are morally offensive to one or both of you, it is up to the spouse doing business to get the locale changed. You don't have to like all of your business associates; by the same token, even an employer should not demand loyalty beyond the boundaries of personal beliefs. In cases like these, there's *always* an alternative.

Leon Botstein, president of Bard College, and his wife, Barbara Haskell, curator for sculpture and painting at New York's Whitney Museum of American Art, are a couple who have achieved recognition unusually early in life. They are acutely coordinated when it comes to each other's sensitivities.

"The trouble is that most people make the mistake of dissembling in public," Botstein says. "My family were Holocaust survivors. I was once asked to have a former high-ranking Nazi to my home because he was interested in making a sizable donation to the college. I told the trustees that I would not pretend to be someone I wasn't. While I didn't go out of my way to make the potential donor uncomfortable, there was no disguising the situation. That's what my father advised, too. As it turned out, we received the donation and I felt that I could live with myself in good conscience."

"On the other hand," remarks Barbara, "I would never attend a business function at a club, with or without Leon, where he would have to use *my name*."

Jerry Della Femina remembers when a major advertising client hosted a dinner in Alabama at which George Wallace was the guest of honor. "Everyone else ran up to the governor, bowing and scraping. I just sat in my seat. It cost me in terms of business, but I had to be true to my own feelings about the man."

If it's the associate or client who causes the offense by making insulting or socially inappropriate remarks to an accompanying spouse, you also have an immediate obligation to bring the discussion back to the matter at hand—business. A couple who communicates effectively can let one another know when the situation is becoming unbearable. If either of you senses big trouble brewing, call the occasion to a close, even if it means facing an awkward phone call or additional encounter. You and your partner should prepare a conversation "code" that permits an inoffensive withdrawal. An impatient baby sitter or an early breakfast meeting is, if underplayed, usually an effective verbal cipher.

Jim Cusick feels strongly that "loyalty should be to each other and the family before any kind of business. Men and women who marry people of different backgrounds from their own must be aware that these types of conflicts will come up—and you'd better have your priorities straight."

Then there are times when social conflicts arise from a spouse's professional rather than moral code of ethics. "My husband knows that I'm not allowed to give political opinions in public," Barbara Walters explains. "He goes to California fund-raisers for various candidates and I don't go to those functions with him. Merv understands and accepts that."

Secretary of Labor Elizabeth Dole takes an equally strong stand. "Public service is a public trust where loyalties run to the people as a whole, and not to one individual. Throughout my years in Washington, I have worked to avoid even the appearance of a conflict of interest or an impropriety."

McCall's columnist and author Charlotte Ford believes that a couple must have mutual respect for each other's feelings. "You should be able to say to your spouse, 'Honey, I just can't handle it this time.' A husband or wife can't expect one another to drop important business associates who were in place before the marriage, but neither should people pressure each other to come along if the company or locale is going to be personally offensive. You must communicate honestly with your mate; sometimes professional couples find this very difficult."

Ford, married to businessman and art collector Edward R. Downe, Jr., also believes that each member of a working couple should be able to attend business functions alone. "I'm perfectly happy to have my husband go by himself— I'm uncomfortable when Ed works the room and there's no one there for me to talk with. On the other hand, there are times when we go to dinners together which I'd rather not attend—you just have to swallow hard."

Even if a couple is mutually supportive, one spouse may not be as ready for professional mixing as the other would hope. Jim Cusick remembers being at a corporate function where a top executive began his swift road downward— because of the immature behavior of his *fifth* wife.

"She was too sexily dressed for the spouse of a senior officer at a conservative company," Jim remembers. "Her behavior wasn't terribly modest, either. She couldn't handle making the rounds. Shortly afterwards, he was told to clear out. I think they really loved each other—as far as I know, they're still together. He just shouldn't have brought her along until she was ready."

LIGHTS, CAMERA, COORDINATION

As Power Partners, one or both of you will be called upon to give an on-record opinion about anything from your field of expertise to your spouse's chocolate mousse. The situation may start out innocuously—you're at a gala museum opening and the local TV station asks each of you for your opinion on the exhibition. You say, "American art is undervalued by most collectors."

Your spouse screws up his face and replies to the rolling camera, "But, honey, the Philadelphia Museum of Art just paid over two million bucks for a crummy Hopper. How can you say that?"

Or one of you is presenting a paper on the relative merits of nuclear and natural gas energy. As a scientist, you are basing your opinions on fact. Later, your spouse, a well-known energy stock fund manager, is asked to comment on your talk. Not wanting to irritate a lucrative client, he inadvertently tells a financial reporter that you're not privy to certain statistics which could affect the future gas market.

Even using different surnames doesn't keep either of you immune from possible embarrassment. Leah, a labor lawyer and faculty member of a major business school, is married to Bart, a management trouble-shooter whose clients are not always pro-union. She remembers the time she had to debate one of her husband's clients on a local radio program.

"It was extremely awkward. Naturally, he had no idea who I was married to, since I work under my maiden name. Bart and I talked it over in advance. We both decided that if either of us were challenged, we would 'fess up, but not before. Fortunately, his firm went along with our decision, and we sneaked through. But I wouldn't want to do that again."

During this period, Leah and Bart were having huge arguments over the renovation of their house, as well as coping with their daughter's "terrible twos." But neither stress source stopped them from remembering their personal partnering priorities; it never occurred to either of them to let the other down in the professional arena.

Debra J. Thomas, director of public information for Bryn Mawr College, was once engaged in conversation with a recent acquaintance at the University of Pennsylvania, where her husband, Paul J. Korshin, is professor of English.

"He made some disparaging remarks about Paul, and then asked me if I knew him." She laughs. "I told him that I knew Dr. Korshin quite well and disagreed with his opinion."

Later, someone filled the newcomer in on Debra and Paul's relationship. "He came storming back to me. 'That was a terrible thing to do—I never would have made those comments if I'd known who you were!' I countered by telling him that he would have then been guilty of concealing the truth. That silenced him quickly enough."

Think of yourselves as a high-wire act. You want to be the one who pulls off the triple somersault, but without a dependable catcher, you won't make it back to the other side of the tent. Let your catching partner know how vital he or she is at your moment under the lights. And don't depend upon the flimsy net of public goodwill. Whenever possible, brief your mate in advance about what will be asked of you. Try and decide beforehand where to draw lines about sharing information with strangers.

"Marilyn Quayle knows how to be a good, supportive backdrop," says Letitia Baldrige. "She's willing to take a backseat and give herself up for her husband's opportunities. I think that husbands have to learn how to do the same for their wives. We should all think in terms of 'us' instead of 'you and me.' "

Of her own supposed sacrifices, Quayle herself has said, "If it weren't for what we did, going to Congress, going to the Senate, I'd still be a small-time lawyer in Huntington, Indiana. I obviously gave up a legal career, but the other opportunities I've had just totally made up for that. And I didn't look at the bad side of things anyway. I make the best out of whatever happens, and I teach my children to do the same thing."

Some couples can handle public disagreements with ease. In fact, they claim that it adds a positive dimension to the marriage. Pat and Jim Schroeder are among them.

"All during law school, it was 'There go the Schroeders again!' " Pat smiles. "Couples who say they always agree when it comes to work or politics are phonies. It's not uncommon at all in Washington. Look at Bob and Elizabeth Dole—they've debated each other in public."

Elizabeth Dole told us about why they chose to air their

differences in a public forum. "Bob and I do agree on the vast majority of issues. As two thinking people, however, we don't march in lockstep, and there are occasions where we 'agree to disagree.'

"Bob and I publicly debated an issue—on the 'Good Morning America' television show! Bob and I took opposite sides in the debate over the creation of a Consumer Protection Agency. We agreed to the debate because we saw it as an opportunity to help inform the public on an important issue that was soon to be voted on in the Congress."

TOGETHERNESS TACTICS

Power Partners are both admired and envied. A tough Chicago commodities trader put it like this: "If those around you see the strength of your marriage—how supportive each of you is of the other—some of the crowd is bound to become envious. I should know. I'm the only female trader in my firm who has a husband waiting for me with job strategies and the occasional salmon soufflé. My size-six supervisor is always trying to steal him, and not for the company." She grins. "I've often wondered how good a concert violinist would be at predicting coffee futures. Actually, my own's not half bad!"

Being a public person means competing—for everything. Jobs, money, recognition, security—the center seat on the dais or two on the aisle. Twosomes are exhilarating and threatening. That's why it's critical never to wear your Power Partnership on your sleeve. Too much togetherness can make those who don't have it uncomfortable. Boyd Matson knows that his wife, NBC executive Betty Hudson, doesn't have to walk around with him all evening. "It's usually my world, too," says TV anchor Matson, "so I want to spend some time talking with whoever is there as well. We're used to sweating out boring evenings together without constantly being in each other's sight. From time to time, we'll meet behind a potted palm and share a quick laugh or moment of gossip."

True Power Partners are strong forces, even when temporarily separated. As we've already admonished, it's up to each spouse to help the other shine and maneuver—after that, each of you should be capable of carrying the ball as an individual.

Your unique partnership will reinforce your own ability to solo. Barbara Lamont, an extraordinary woman who owns New Orleans' Channel 49, WCCL-TV, and an additional satellite facility, is married to Ludwig Gelobter, a former stockbroker who now runs a successful import operation called Freight Finders. This mid-life couple has an offbeat but solid relationship that has withstood differences in background (she's an African-American of French and South American descent; he's a Polish Jew who hid from the Nazis as a child) and 180-degree career swings. At various times, each has been the primary care-giver to their three children. Each has "taken turns" contributing the bulk of the family upkeep. What keeps them anchored to each other is love and a pair of rugged cellular phones.

Barbara knows that their style is highly atypical. "We're always apart. Even our finances are pretty separate—whoever has the credit card out first usually pays! Even our kids thought we were a bit strange. I spent a good part of their childhood running the Nigerian national broadcasting system or singing in clubs around the world. But I think that no matter how strong each of us is alone, we're better together. It's more than missing him—I really notice a difference in the way I act. We're both highly independent, but we need that contact no matter where each of us happens to be."

It's this hidden difference that makes the most successful two-career couples so formidable. Clutching each other's arm or coyly holding hands projects an *insecure* image. So does the response "I'll have to talk to my spouse before I can answer that question." Power Partners exude a more elusive sort of social security.

"It's the Noah's Ark of the 1990s," concludes newspaper columnist and Fox Television interviewer Cindy Adams, herself half of a longtime dynamic duo as the wife of comic Joey

Adams. "There's nothing more dazzling than a couple who has everything—including each other. There's no vulnerability."

Even if you and your spouse don't have *everything* (and no one really does, despite Robin Leach's drippingly persuasive plaudits), your co-mentoring powers will make you feel as though you wanted for nothing and could face anyone across a table or a microphone. In becoming more socially adept, you'll both realize that having unquestioning backup is the most precious social asset of all. No matter where you go, or how often you have to justify yourself, there's someone *on*—if not always at—your side. As with all valuable assets, you must learn to appreciate its worth and become steadfast guardians of its surety.

4

CLUBHOUSE CONDUCT

♦

The idea of inviting career colleagues to your home is simultaneously potent and terrifying. Potent, because you and your spouse can be in full control—the food, the theme, the guest list, the style of dress. Terrifying, because you may be inviting guests whose impressions could have strong bearings on your futures. Old friends will easily forgive fallen soufflés and flat jokes; the new department chairman and his killer-lawyer wife may not be so charitable.

While most etiquette experts feel that deal-making and dinner parties don't mix, they offer vast amounts of practical information about prepping the scene for a successful merging of business with pleasure. Which is why we're not going to go into the nuances of place settings and menus; there are already enough books on those subjects. We assume that Power Partners will offer the best that their budgets allow when it comes to edibles, potables, and the plates and glasses that hold them.

What canny co-mentors want to know is how to carry off the kind of party that will enhance their reputations and open doors without looking like social orangutans. Lest you and your spouse find this too calculating, consider the findings of Seagram's *Crown Royal Report on American Entertaining*.

This study, published in late 1989, was based on a nationwide telephone survey of 1,001 people aged twenty-one through fifty-nine with household incomes over $25,000.

It found that 30 percent of those who attend social events in people's homes hope to create new business opportunities for themselves, a noticeably higher percentage figure than for individuals seeking romantic encounters. One in seven participants indicated that they had made business deals at social events—a highly motivated group the survey identifies as calculating partygoers.

Women enjoy conducting deals and nurturing contacts nearly as much as men, although they do prefer making the rounds with a spouse in tow. And parties-with-a-purpose tend to bring couples closer together, even if there's a significant amount of work and planning involved.

According to the survey, ambitious couples consider home entertaining an important part of their lifestyle and are frequently willing to spend ample amounts of time and money on making their habitats as welcoming as possible.

Their zeal comes from a genuine sense of pleasure. Only 6 percent of those polled admitted to entertaining simply out of a sense of obligation. Most dual careerists like getting together with like-minded associates and feel that there's nothing wrong with a little TCB between courses. The trouble begins when "taking care of business" takes over to the point where the two of you lose control.

THE SEVEN DEADLY SINS OF SOCIALIZING

1. *Not Showing Up at Your Own Party*. Unbelievable? Ridiculous? Judith and Peter Price, prominent New York media executives, were reported to have once done precisely that. These aggressive entertainers invited dozens of beautiful people to their posh digs for a black-tie bash. Guests reported that the food

and wine were plentiful and delicious, but that it was virtually impossible to thank their hosts, who spent much of the evening elsewhere, preferring a last-minute invite from Malcolm Forbes to their own hospitality.

2. *Failing to Coordinate Plans with Your Partner.* Barbara Lamont and Ludwig Gelobter each invited one hundred associates for open house—each thinking that the other spouse was still away on business. "Somehow we managed," recalls Barbara. "I don't think the caterer enjoyed it very much. Thank God for New York's late-night delis!"

   Charlotte Ford insists on "discussing plans with your partner from the beginning, especially the guest list. Two-career couples are at a terrible time disadvantage. It's hard enough organizing your daily routines when both of you work. With any kind of party, advance planning is best because there are always last-minute crises. And don't forget to keep your sense of humor, because something can always go wrong."

3. *Letting Children Be Heard More Than Seen.* Out of the mouths of babes come all sorts of business tips and tidbits. One food marketing strategist recalls the time when his precocious at-home product tester Timothy, age eleven, gleefully told a potential competitor's wife all about "how smart Daddy is to launch that new candy bar right before Halloween." The enthusiastic youngster even dragged his pretty new friend upstairs for a sample.

4. *Neglecting to Weed Out Would-Be Troublemakers.* A low-key executive will never forget the night that he invited his personal lawyer to help "round out" a gathering of his spouse's data research colleagues. As it happened, her project partner's husband was also a lawyer—one who helped clients sue their legal representatives for malpractice! "I finally had to place myself between them with a serving cart. It

wasn't exactly the kind of live entertainment we had in mind."

5. *Overpitching Your Party's Purpose.* If the invitation says "Please join us for a festive fall brunch," guests have a right *not* to expect a rapid-fire recitative on the merits of your favorite charity or the attributes of your spouse's dandy new invention. Fund-raisers are fine places to mingle, but you'll cause nothing but resentment if you disguise an out-and-out sales meeting as a cozy get-together.

6. *Putting Guests to Work Without Warning.* A pair of self-made, affluent entrepreneurs think there's nothing more fun than a "do-it-yourself" affair where unsuspecting invitees, usually dressed in expensive finery, are immediately put to work as scullery maids and handymen. We're not talking about clearing a few dishes or helping out behind the bar. How about peeling and chopping vegetables, marinating meats, boning fishes, hauling wood or charcoal (depending upon the season) up from the basement? And, of course, after dessert and brandy, taking out the garbage!

   With all the money these hosts have saved, you would think that they'd surprise their regulars with a lavish end-of-year Caribbean cruise for all of that effort. Unfortunately, there never *are* any regulars after first-time guests' cleaning bills come in.

7. *Encouraging Party Pyrotechnics.* The intimate dinner party, be the attire casual or black tie, can be fraught with hidden social snares. Here is where colleagues and even friends get the chance to size each other up —elbow to eyeball—for three-hour stretches with nothing between them except a few inches of table. Astute Power Partners know the value of such close encounters. A positive impression garnered at such gatherings can last a lifetime. But beware hosts who like to baste the roast with conversational friction.

   Some couples are so proud of their argumentative prowess that they'll go through great pains to provoke their visitors at every turn. During New York's notorious Robert Chambers/Jennifer Levin "preppie" murder trial, an unwitting couple found themselves at an intimate dinner party where the cocktail hour activity consisted of husbands tying up their spouses' wrists with underwear (thoughtfully supplied by the hostess) to see if Chambers could have "accidentally" killed Levin.

As if this wasn't stimulating enough, mealtime heralded a full-scale forum over the results of the exercise; ladies took the victim's side while the gentlemen clung fiercely to the notion of Chambers's possible innocence. All gentlemen, that is, except for the male half of our hapless pair. Himself a crime reporter, he quietly explained the rules of evidence to the bellicose crowd. His wife, a highly regarded cardiologist, smiled in gratitude at her husband's collected approach to cooling off the lynch mob atmosphere.

Six months later, this same reporter was up for a plum position at a major network. His appointment to the on-air news team was virtually assured. As he entered the office of the station manager, he realized he'd seen that face before—across the table at that memorable dinner. The station manager remembered, too. "Carl, I know everyone thinks you're a real pistol, but I'll never hire any man who allows himself to be dominated in public by his wife. Get the hell out of here!" (Happily, Carl ended up with the same job at a rival station paying thirty grand more a year.)

Religion, politics, and sex are topics that have *highly limited* places at the table. If the gathering consists of people who know each other well, these topics can add zest when presented in moderate portions. But never serve them up to a group of relative strangers or you'll end up with a serious case of social botulism.

CREATING A MASTERFUL GUEST MIX

So long as you both stay away from the seven blunder zones, be as creative or traditional as you please. Keep in mind *why* you're giving this fete in the first place. If any kind of business is involved, who's going to be there should be at the top of your party planning list.

What most people remember the day after are the guests. A perfect steak au poivre doesn't score nearly as high in the memory bank as passing petit fours to Jerry Hall or sipping spritzers with Jim Robinson. If you can't persuade the *New York Post*'s Page Six or *Fortune* magazine regulars to appear, you can usually count on acceptances from some of the more successful and dynamic solos and duos in your own circle.

Letitia Baldrige believes that hosts shouldn't be afraid to mix guests of different ages, occupations, and interests. If you've ever been the lone software designer or literature professor plunked down in the midst of thirty corporate lawyers or investment bankers, you'll definitely agree with this philosophy.

She always suggests explaining who people are when you introduce them. "Use logic when breaking the ice. Bring a fellow executive over to a client, or introduce a peer to a peer in another company. Entertaining is a powerful tool that must be wielded with care."

Peter W. Prescott, entertaining and special projects editor for *Food & Wine* magazine, thinks it's unfair to "impose on friends to bolster a business deal dinner." On the other hand, he heartily supports the concept of keeping the action lively.

"There are no dos and don'ts anymore about intermingling. I always like a few scandalous guests, so long as they don't turn into troublemakers."

George Green and Wilma Jordan admit that they "like to bring people together who do well."

Explains George, "There are no secrets in our world about spouses. Lots of people come to parties in order to meet the other partner. Many executives do it all the time. It's to be expected—we're public figures in business and publishing circles. In fact, if it's a small dinner party, I usually let everyone know who'll be in attendance. You'd be surprised how few dropouts we get!"

But he also believes in setting up business-cum-social introductions with delicacy. "Make sure that individuals want to be invited. Don't just call out of the blue. Set the scene with a lunch or drink in advance. It's de facto that colleagues can become friends—just take it slowly."

Adds Wilma, "If you really don't like someone, forget getting involved. And if you're inviting relatively new contacts or associates, be sure to brief *each other* before the party begins."

Sometimes a social disaster threatens in spite of taking every polite precaution. But they don't always work out for the worst.

Stephen and Fredrica Friedman once invited the South African consul general and the chairman of the African-American Institute to the same party. Unbeknownst to the affable hosts, that particular consul had been the very individual who had denied the other gentleman his recent visa request. Instead of trying to keep them at opposite ends of the room, the Friedmans let nature take its course, relying upon the overall atmosphere of camaraderie. The two sides got a chance to talk away from their usual heated arena; the chairman's visa came through.

When potential problem partygoers don't play by diplomatic rules, it's not a faux pas to take one (or both) of the following steps:

- Bring whichever poised combatant you know better into a private corner and explain that you had no idea that the other person would cause discomfort. A sincere apology makes it easier for you to prevail upon his or her good sense and taste for the duration. Better a silent standoff than verbal or physical fisticuffs at the buffet table.

- Enlist another guest to promote détente. At one of our own recent open houses, a famous columnist was on the verge of baring her claws to a popular TV actor who happened to be of Irish descent. Before the smoldering words caught fire, we steered the otherwise amiable guest in the direction of a sportswriter who happened to be an expert on Gaelic football. The helpful colleague kept the unwary thespian occupied until the columnist departed.

If all else fails to lower the emotional thermostat, the host has a right to ask one or both of the offending guests to beat a hasty retreat. When intoxication is part of the problem, a considerate couple will call a cab or get someone leaving at the same time to make sure the visitor gets home safely.

GUEST STYLES OF THE RICH AND FAMOUS

Fredrica Friedman enjoys inviting her many noted authors to mix it up with her husband's Wall Street colleagues and their spouses. "I treat them like everyone else. I'll take an author who's just gotten back from Paris and escort him over to another person who may have some common interests. I'll get the conversation rolling by saying something like 'You were just in Paris—Jason lived there for five years, but I don't think he's been back recently. Mr. Well-Known Writer has been telling me about the wonderful new show at the Louvre, and I know how much you love Titian. . . .'"

Celebrated guests must never be invited for the sole function of demonstrating their talents. You wouldn't expect a painter to arrive, easel in hand, or a novelist to drag along galleys of his latest thriller. Actors, musicians, composers, and dancers are there for the same reasons everyone else is—

to meet new people and perhaps make a useful contact or two.

Doctors and other high-level service professionals are fairly used to being asked for on-the-spot consultations. But that doesn't mean you and your spouse should encourage this any more than you would a fellow guest to badger a concert pianist into an impromptu recital. Gently rescue the put-upon party by saying, "I hate to break in, but Ms. Johnson is leaving soon and I do know how much you wanted to meet her." Safer still: "We're about to serve dessert in the other room—I don't want either of you to miss my chocolate surprise!" Then, escort both guests away, changing the topic of conversation as you stroll.

What about the honored guest who requires constant coddling? While most celebrities enjoy social events that give them the chance to melt into the rest of the crowd, there are those who require a constant spotlight or they regress to their terrible twos. You can usually spot them quickly because they advertise their entrance with the subtlety of neon.

The spouse of a prominent CEO, known for her delightfully relaxed entertaining style, remembers one discomfiting incident.

"We were having our usual mix of my husband's senior staff and the people from my antique-buying business. There was a new couple—a charming gentleman who had just been promoted to vice president of sales and his attractive wife. She was a leading network soap opera star. Unfortunately, most of the other guests didn't follow daytime TV, so no one knew her by name or face. She practically demanded everyone ask for her autograph. This prima donna refused to leave her husband's side, which made it virtually impossible for *my* husband to introduce him to other higher-ups in the firm. I also had the unenviable task of keeping her from destroying some potential sales opportunities among my friends. I felt sorry for this young VP—he could control everything except his wife's boorish behavior."

If the egocentric party pooper is a guest of honor, your role is, as with outside business functions, to grin and make it bearable for everyone else. However, if the unwanted center of attention isn't the primary reason for the gathering, treat him or her as you would other unwelcome callers. As hosts, your main obligation is to keep the majority enjoying itself.

ENTERTAINING WITH AGENDAS

Georgette Mosbacher, chief executive of La Prairie cosmetics and spouse to the U.S. secretary of commerce, believes that, used properly, one's home can be an ideal place to conduct professional affairs. "In a world of faceless corporations, I find the personal touch lacking," she admitted in a *New York Times* "home entertaining" supplement. "A lot of people never meet the CEO of the corporation with whom they are doing business. I think people like coming to one's home—particularly in my business, where the personal is very important."

She often holds luncheons for major store managers—invitations are extended by telephone, with follow-up written RSVP requests. For more formal occasions, Ms. Mosbacher also bends a few time-honored etiquette rules.

"I don't serve ladies first. We go around the table in order. And if it's a two-career couple, I try to seat the husband and wife together, because they never get to see each other except at dinner."

Hattie Winston and Harold Wheeler agree that home is often the best place to encourage enterprise, provided everyone knows about the agenda in advance.

"We're known for throwing parties for professional purposes," says Harold. "Hattie has helped start up several successful companies for other people."

Hattie explains. "A friend of ours was getting started in the decorating field. He did our apartment, which we thought turned out rather nicely. I held a dinner to introduce him to some of our acquaintances who might well become clients.

"There was nothing ambiguous in the invitation. We

told everyone that we wanted to show off our new decor, and that the decorator himself would be present. I did the same sort of thing recently for another friend who puts gift baskets together."

The pair stress that it's crucial not to pressure either the person "on show" or the rest of the company. "We even used to hold salons where less experienced actors and musicians than ourselves could try out their talents. In your own home, you can be up front," emphasizes Hattie.

Jerry Della Femina tells of one especially deceitful host who wasn't.

"My wife, Judy Licht, and I were out at our weekend house. Everyone who knows us is aware that we're uncomfortable talking business at parties. A friend of ours invited us over to his house for Saturday lunch. He told us that the gathering would be a small one—just a few couples. He mentioned something about a politician from another part of the country.

"As Judy and I drove up, we noticed a guard at the front door. As it turned out, *we* were the only guests—besides our host (without his wife) and the politician. The agenda was for me to turn this man into a viable candidate for president of the United States! I didn't even know who the guy was. For two hours, we had to sit there and listen to his image problems. We didn't even get the lunch we were invited for."

It's those who don't understand the real value of socializing away from desks and meeting rooms who make the worst social blunders. With time being today's most precious professional commodity, even the traditional professional lunch can't take the place of a leisurely dinner or Sunday-afternoon tea; the latter are still the best way of getting people to open up and share more of themselves.

Cathie Black, publisher of *USA Today*, agrees. In *The Wall Street Journal Book of Chief Executive Style*, she states, "I would probably say to a young person who is very ambitious, male or female, 'the more things that make you comfortable with people, they are all little notches that help.' "

Working couples who enjoy hosting have the distinct

advantage of being able to create an automatic atmosphere of being "at ease." Associates look at their bosses and peers with a new sense of humanity—you're not *just* going to the home of the man or woman who signs the paychecks or the client who has agreed to let you represent the product. You are spending the afternoon or evening with two people who have graciously invited you to partake of their private personas.

If there is an agenda, open or otherwise, it still behooves you to keep on your social guard. But getting together as couples enables you to gather useful private and professional information. Now that you know Thad's wife is a corporate loan officer, you'll think twice about making jokes about greedy, thieving bank executives.

As cold-blooded as the workaday world continues to be, it *is* more difficult to dump on people with whom you socialize. Nothing enhances a couple's reputation faster than becoming known for giving a good party.

FIVE PARTY POSITIVES FOR PROFESSIONAL COUPLES

1. *Make every guest feel welcome and wanted.* If the guest list isn't completely your doing, summon up your strongest Pollyanna attitude and play the part. A few years ago, when a night on the political banquet circuit unexpectedly brought a dozen younger executives back to the home of media baron Rupert Murdoch, the host made everyone feel on equal footing by serving the drinks himself.

    When the list is up to you and your spouse, stick to this unbreakable rule: NEVER INVITE ANYONE YOU DON'T LIKE INTO YOUR HOME. If you don't want someone around, you won't be able to make them or yourselves feel truly comfortable. You'll always be compensating for your true feelings in some way—and it *will* show.

2. *Act naturally.* Be your best selves, to be sure, but don't put on artificial airs if your style differs from that of

Malcolm Forbes. Only the worst sort of climbers scrutinize the furniture and the silver. Money has very little to do with successful entertaining; creativity and hospitality are what counts.

Letitia Baldrige likes to point out that even if you don't have Chippendale chairs and Old Masters on the wall, there's nothing to stop you from concocting a lavish-looking and -tasting traditional meal . . . if that's your dining preference. She encourages using celebrity recipes (almost all magazines have features on Food Favorites of the Famous and Famished). If a dish doesn't quite work, you can always blame it on Pat Buckley or Luciano Pavarotti.

David Siegal, a former vice president at a major brokerage firm, now a private caterer, thinks that younger executive couples too often get caught up in the "one-upsmanship" game.

"I remember an ambitious pair who kept referring to me as 'our private chef.' They had a two-bedroom apartment. Instead of doing a gracious buffet for sixteen or twenty, they insisted on packing the limited floor space. No one could move or enjoy their dinner. You can always tell who's really interested in showing guests a good time or just showing off. When I present a menu, I always say, 'If you want to dazzle, I can give you pretentious trash, or I can serve you a really tasty, appropriate dinner.' "

Take extra care if you are entertaining your immediate boss or other superiors in your firm. This is no time to show off or serve up false humility. Don't attempt anything that you've never tried before. Show respect and err, if at all, on the conservative side where food, liquor, and atmosphere are concerned. Never brag about private social conquests at the office.

3. *Woo business contacts with care.* One usually clever couple had spent a week preplanning their joint assault on a venture fund director and his wife. As soon

as the pair arrived, the husband whisked the director's wife over to the most lionized person at the party. His spouse made certain that the director, a serious amateur chef, was able to observe the intricate workings of the Chinese catering team. The male host kept making positive remarks about the director; his partner continuously praised the community service efforts of the director's wife.

By the evening's end, the pair was exhausted but certain that the effort would result in substantial backing for the husband's new magazine. Nothing happened.

What the hosting partners hadn't known was that the courted couple were barely on speaking terms—with each other! The only results of their diligence was a tasteless pass made at the hostess by the footloose venture fund director.

4. *Keep the mood appropriately festive.* You haven't invited these people here to submit them to additional pressures and stresses. Nor should you and your spouse feel put-upon by playing host. Whether everyone's wearing jeans or ballroom attire, it's up to the two of you to set the tone.

   Nothing sends successful professionals away in droves faster than the disquieting feeling of being back in the office. Your living room, kitchen, or terrace may well prove to be hospitable hatcheries for new deals and connections. But save the slog work for future meetings. If the start of something big gets brewing, shake hands, and get back to circulating. Don't sequester yourselves in the bedroom while everyone else is relaxing and getting to know each other on lighter levels. By locking yourself (or selves) away, you may miss other golden opportunities coming through your very own doors.

5. *Be as good a guest as you are a host.* Whether or not it creates a climate for self-promotion, the successful party is a skillful means to future invitations. Some

couples, though impeccable, delightful hosts under their own roofs, instantly ignore every social nicety when it comes to being guests.

An established public relations woman with her own firm recalls how shocked she was at the behavior of her former favorite hosts. "I had been to so many wonderful dinner parties at this couple's Georgetown home. They always made me feel comfortable with their congressional friends, even though we had little in common. They were quite rich, but they never showed off by serving anything too fancy or asking us to dress up. I always looked forward to seeing them when I was in Washington.

"When they moved to New York, I was thrilled at the chance of paying them back for all those great evenings. You can imagine my feelings when they showed up two hours late at a party I gave specifically in their honor. Not only that, but they insulted one of my new clients, an extremely shy young actress who isn't used to people buttonholing her about her sexual and political preferences. The husband even had the audacity to go into the kitchen and yell at my housekeeper for not putting enough dressing on the salad. Their incredible behavior has made me really think twice about keeping them as friends."

LOYALTY LOVES COMPANY

Being socially loyal to personal and professional friends is always a winning trait. Just because someone has had a losing year in the market or lost a key position is no reason to cross their names off your list of regulars. Power Partners are often more sensitive to such situations because of their unswerving loyalty to each other. Such guests are usually grateful for the opportunity to show that they're ready for the next round. This is one instance where promoting a guest is good form.

Let's say that your good friend, Karen, has just been laid

off as a stockbroker. Those in the field know that layoffs have far more to do with market slumps than skill. Take Karen over to your husband's brokerage partner. You begin the introduction like this: "Mitchell, I want you to meet Karen. Karen just left her firm—she's a specialist in pharmaceutical stocks. Where should she be looking?" That's all. No pressure to hire—just a neutral opening gambit. But when Karen gets back on her feet, she'll remember your helpful tactical moves on her behalf. When you've just lost your three biggest retail clients to a competitor, she'll be there with cocktails and leads for you.

Jim Cusick, who was once abruptly fired from a senior post at CBS, agrees. "When something like that happens, you really learn fast who your friends are. To this day, Gail and I remember who dropped us and who didn't!"

GUESTING GAMES: ICEBREAKERS OR NUTCRACKERS?

While many etiquette experts agree that organized activities can be the perfect way to combat shyness or sluggish conversation flow, it takes confident, experienced hosts to keep such diversions and contests from becoming a means to an end . . . of the party!

With the coming of the VCR and fact-figuring games like Trivial Pursuit, casual evenings spent with people who are familiar with each other's personalities and backgrounds are often enhanced by introducing a round of video Clue or, more traditionally, bridge or Monopoly. Groups like these can make jokes at each other's expense or tease one another without incurring much lasting damage. For them, winning is merely part of the evening's pleasure—not a measure of their own worthiness or business skills.

The only problem that might arise in such a gathering is if a new member of the social circle does not share the group's enthusiasm or interest. Some individuals have strong psychological feelings about even the most innocuous amusements.

Dr. Zussman believes that "some people are vulnerable

to any kind of self-exposure. It may be rooted in early fears about 'being shown up.' At my son's twenty-fifth high school reunion, part of the day's program was a casual game of baseball. All of the men reverted back to their sixteen-year-old selves. One man, who had deliberately chosen a different career path from that of his famous father, refused to even put on a glove. These anxieties can run surprisingly deep."

Others are afraid that word or knowledge games will make them appear ignorant to others. Obviously, no good host would spring an evening of bridge (or poker) without advance warning at invitation time. One of us remembers a tedious evening where married hosts attempted to teach the intricacies of contract bridge to a largely disinterested group of guests. They ended up squabbling over the best way to impart their unwanted information.

For small, informal get-togethers, the best policy is to let people know that a certain game may be part of the proceedings. That gives the guest several options. He or she can either accept with pleasure, bow out gracefully, or accept and admit a lack of skill or familiarity with the activity. The hosts can then offer pointers in advance, or can ease their minds about the seriousness of the activity to come. "Don't worry—none of us is very good. We just do this for fun. We only play for about an hour while we serve coffee and seconds on dessert."

At larger, more organized events, getting-to-know-you is frequently the objective of such games. Letitia Baldrige commends a young Florida hostess who gave each guest a number. Several people had the same number. During the course of the party, the idea was that those with the identical numbers were supposed to congregate and see how much they had in common. The group with the most similarities won.

While this sounds like a perfectly charming, harmless idea of an icebreaker, today's "small world" reality could still cause trouble.

One Philadelphia society couple tried a similar tactic at an "at home" charity ball. Couples were given different kinds of flowers as they walked in the door. Those with the same bloom were to see how many ways their paths had crossed. Since most had identical backgrounds, the hosts thought that this was a clever way of reinforcing the party's theme of "Remembrance of Things Past."

For the first hour or so, all one heard was the polite rustle of satin pouf skirts and the tinkle of champagne flutes. Suddenly, an audible gasp could be heard from the elegant, book-lined study. Two of the couples in the carnation bunch had discovered that one gentleman, head of the admissions board of a local university, had rejected another couple's daughter. Fortunately, a quick intervention by the composed hosting wife smoothed things out.

Games that work best with large numbers of people meeting for the first time involve an activity where everyone has an equal chance of winning or making a meaningful contribution.

Peter W. Prescott recalls a memorable treasure hunt at a friend's country home. "There were around thirty of us. Teams of five or six were assigned to cars. It was a beautiful day, and the hosts had really gone to a lot of trouble to create imaginative clues. No one really cared who came in first. I don't even remember the prize. What I do remember was how well I got to know the others in my car and how much fun we had figuring out where to look next."

Scavenger hunts are also enjoyable, weather and time permitting. Obviously, these kinds of games are more suited to parties with a suburban or rural setting. It would be unfair to ask guests to run around downtown Chicago, Dallas, or New York in search of obscure items. If you and your spouse find this entertainment concept appealing, be sure to let your neighbors in on the fun so that they are prepared when strangers ring their bells requesting a polka dot bow tie or a loan of their child's Smurf doll. Guests should always announce themselves as part of the Joneses' party. It's also the hosts' responsibility to be certain that everyone gets their items back in good condition.

There's nothing odd about this adolescent zeal for playing "let's pretend." A recent survey found that in households with $75,000-plus incomes, one of the most popular excuses for adult get-togethers is Halloween. Other popular dates for party-giving include the Super Bowl, St. Patrick's Day, and Mardi Gras.

One professional party planner thinks that "people are looking for the chance to show their creativity and uniqueness. Games and themes allow for individuality and playfulness. That extends to what hosts are serving, too. It's not enough just to use expensive ingredients and liquor—you have to have special cocktails and wines, mineral waters, and coordinated cuisine. Of course, when the party is primarily for doing business, I try and steer clients toward moderation. But even the stuffiest CEOs get a kick out of a whimsical touch like a portrait sketch artist or a fortune teller."

Letitia Baldrige recalls a party where a clown in full makeup circulated among the guests, revealing surprisingly accurate facts about their lives. "What they did not know was that he was actually one of their good friends."

Again, she urges care when employing the services of a professional entertainer without checking out his or her act in advance. "Someone you might think is hilarious in a nightclub might well prove to be embarrassing in your living room," she cautions. One of last year's New York mayoral candidates learned this the hard way when he drew upon the services of popular comedian Jackie Mason to help raise money and votes. The comic's blunt delivery made the politician look racist and unsympathetic. Oh, yes, he lost.

John and Ellie Raynolds are avid party-givers who enjoy more interactive forms of diversion. They often conduct their guests through Outward Bound bonding exercises.

"We like to have many people over to our apartment at one time," John, Outward Bound's energetic president, explains. "People end up sitting around or inside our Jacuzzi and everywhere else. Sometimes I invite one of my Outward Bound staff to help get the activities going. Most people enjoy what Ellie and I plan, but, then, our guests tend to be lively, intelligent types."

One of John's favorite "warm-ups" is a game where everyone stands in a circle on individual pieces of paper. "I then pose questions to the group; anyone who answers affirmatively goes inside the circle. Questions can range from who's got on blue underwear to how many times did you make love that week. Later on, the 'insiders' get to ask questions of their own. Guests usually get into the relaxed and silly spirit of the game."

While you might think that sophisticated business people would use any excuse not to reveal their more intimate selves to strangers, it's another common Outward Bound exercise that sends certain male guests running toward the kitchen and away from the action. "The trust fall does seem to make some men squeamish—women really enjoy dropping back into the two lines of supporting arms," John Raynolds observes.

At more sedate, intimate dinner parties, John and Ellie like to encourage more subtle but equally powerful kinds of social bonding. "We get everyone to hold hands for a brief, personal meditation before eating," says John. "This creates a warm, giving atmosphere where everyone feels that he or she belongs."

Other Raynolds tactics include posing a group question for discussion during mealtime, and short speeches by John in which he highlights the achievements and common interests of each guest in the room. "We try to make people feel special. Parties where the conversation flows in the realm of ideas instead of on a single, work-oriented track—those are the best kinds in terms of making friends and even future professional contacts. No one's showing off or comparing corporate notes. Instead, we're all having fun and exposing ourselves to new ideas.

"I once hosted a colleague who, as a result of participating in some of the Outward Bound routines at one of our parties, decided to join the organization. I got him to leave another prestigious board to come onto ours."

The Raynolds philosophy of creating good business feelings by *not* emphasizing agendas seems to work at even the highest corporate level. "We gave a dinner party in Minneapolis for the head of a major conglomerate. I asked a good CEO friend of ours to assist us in putting together twenty heads of leading Minneapolis companies. They each brought their respective spouses, and all of us had a marvelous time. Everyone had a chance to learn about common problems and goals. We have found that executives from all backgrounds really enjoy letting their guards and hair down. We've had the chairman of Rolls-Royce eat dinner in our oversized empty Jacuzzi."

PARTYGOER (AND GIVER) PRIORITIES

A 1989 study reveals that most people over thirty don't particularly care about formality. Nine in ten individuals polled admitted that most gatherings they attended were casual. Over half didn't think twice about receiving a telephone invitation instead of a formal note. The same held true for postparty decorum. Thank-you notes, it seems, are no longer *de rigueur*. And hardly anyone employed outside help for inside entertaining.

What two-career hosts care most about is providing friends and associates with food and beverages that taste good and an atmosphere that's conducive to opening up and talking.

None of which means that written invitations and thank-yous aren't appreciated. It's simply that the advent of the two-career couple with their limited schedules and full calendars has modified many time-honored customs. For example, it is now permissible for hosts of all ages and incomes to do the following:

- Make use of quality pre-prepared foods, even at a formal occasion. If a guest asks for a recipe, you can smile mysteriously, begging off with the "old family secret" excuse, or, as many urbanites do, brag about the "wonderful new Japanese take-out that makes up tempura and sushi to order." Working couples take pride in sharing such secrets—despite traditional etiquette advice about not enquiring as to the origins of the repast.

- Have guests tend to their own cloakroom chores. For a small group, it's always nice to have someone help you on and off with a coat, but there's nothing rude about expecting large numbers of guests—at an open house or cocktail party—to take care of their own outerwear. A school-age family member might take on the job during the early hours of the event.

- Let guests pitch in with clearing plates and mixing drinks. As noted earlier, this is not the same as assigning full-scale KP duty. But if most of the company know each other and the tone is casual, it's fine to accept an offer of help. If you'd rather do everything yourself, be emphatic but express gratitude, or feelings might be hurt.

- Introduce VCR or TV viewing as part of the event. Just so long as the guests know *in advance* that this is part of your entertainment agenda. If you're holding a large party, chances are that there will be a small group who wish to watch a certain sports event. We've been to black-tie affairs where, during playoff periods, it's not uncommon to see guests grouped around the largest screen on the premises.

One slightly self-conscious young American woman who was attending her first formal London dinner party was amused and surprised when, after coffee was served, all of the female guests, plus one gentleman, stood up in unison and headed toward the hosts' bedroom. After inquiring whether she should join them, the culture-conscious Yank was told, "That depends upon whether you're an 'Upstairs, Downstairs' fanatic!"

ENTERTAIN FOR FUN—AND YOU'LL PROFIT!

Never deceive yourselves that parties are primarily for carrying you up social and professional ladders. If you become too calculating, this veneer of aggressiveness will stick to guests like syrup, and your intentions will backfire. No one enjoys feeling exploited—even with caviar and champagne in hand.

Couples have the entertaining advantage of being able to circulate more efficiently than a single host. The burden of keeping everyone diverted is lessened right from the start. Your broader interest range will likely cover most conversation bases. If your spouse isn't particularly comfortable with the shy personnel director, she can steer you over to their corner. When you find yourself becoming bored with the sales department chief's fly-fishing tall tales, your husband can rescue you and others who would rather compare notes on Tom Clancy's latest thriller.

Just as you do when you're off your own turf, each of you should work to balance out the other's social shortcomings. Power Partners usually enjoy entertaining for all occasions because, as the *Crown Royal Report* suggests, couples look upon party planning as yet another activity that brings them closer together. Although most female partners continue to do much of the cooking, men are taking over in the kitchen in increasing numbers, just as their wives are starting to influence the selection of wine and spirits, a more common male practice.

Think about the last time you and your spouse really had fun at your own party. What do you remember most? Your three-year-old son digging his fingerpaint-stained fingers into the $100 rum cake? The thunderstorm that blew the tent down—on the assemblyman's mother? Or the wonderful new friendship and subsequent business alliance that you forged by inviting your wife's new client?

A successful event is filled with unexpected twists and

turns. Well-tempered teamwork will keep you poised for surprises. Start by treating *each other* as honored guests, and those around you will respond in kind. When you share your good times with others, the party's never over.

· 5 ·

THE HOME TEAM

♦

In her 1989 book, *Champion of the Great American Family*, U.S. congresswoman Pat Schroeder demonstrated both how little and far we've come as a nation in terms of accepting the two-career couple as the norm. Although more than half of American women work outside their homes, she wrote, and despite the fact that companies are becoming sensitive to the parenting and other personal motivations of women *and* men, mixed signals continue to fly in the face of productive family interaction.

Asked to elaborate, the Colorado representative told us, "I'm not sure that two-career couples have made much difference yet. We still have the myth that you can't be a good family man or woman and have a great career. People are afraid of bringing this up. And it doesn't have much to do with foreign companies buying up American businesses, either. Even the Japanese usually bring in an American management team."

Schroeder believes that traditional gender-linked fears have a lot to do with the slowness of change. "Men are afraid that they're going to get stuck with all the work. They're not stupid. They foresee the same professional conflicts that women have. It's even harder for them to plead child care problems—it's easier for those words to come from *our* mouths."

Yet Congresswoman Schroeder and her lawyer husband, Jim, have vital careers, a strong marriage, and seemingly well-adjusted children. They've also survived personal tragedies and public disappointments. All of this *without* many of the societal changes they're both still fighting for. The Schroeders are successful, yes—a superfamily, definitely not.

Arlie Hochschild's provocative book, *The Second Shift*, caused a good deal of controversy when it was published. She and her research assistant tracked the home and work life of fifty Bay Area West Coast couples during the 1980s. Their findings looked pretty gloomy where true marital equality and teamwork were concerned. Her hopes, like Schroeder's, lie in a more progressive attitude on the parts of government and business.

The couples we interviewed, most of them parents, come from a broader geographic and sociological spectrum than Hochschild's. As we have seen, their passion for keeping their careers and relationships in top form is beyond question. These partners approach family life with the same sense of teamwork.

No one would dispute that raising secure and confident children in a two-career home is a challenge. There are ground rules that can't tolerate much bending. Stresses for both parents and kids can emerge without warning. But so can wonderful opportunities and rewarding experiences.

We're going to focus on those last two positives. Pat Schroeder believes that "kids want *wings*, not things. If working mothers and fathers can do roots and substance, it can be phenomenal. The benefits come when the parents interact every day. If you both have careers, there's lots of exciting stuff at the dinner table."

There's "lots of exciting stuff" away from the dinner table, too—if parents are prepared for what lies ahead. As child psychologist and mother Evelyn Sherburne says, "Career couples who want to raise kids need high frustration tolerance, stamina, and a real ability to set priorities and be honest with themselves." In other words, they should strive to be Power Partnering Parents.

Dr. Ann Curtain Ward, a family-oriented psychiatrist and a fellow of the Academy of Psychoanalysis, thinks that two-career couples with healthy relationships have a distinct advantage. "What you have in such marriages are two people who are used to solving problems in their daily lives. They may disagree, but they have also learned the art of flexibility. Children in such households see parents who occasionally argue, but play fair with each other. That's a major plus."

Says French-born PR executive Marie-Claude Stockl, "My husband, Larry, expected me to be more domestic. I'm not into cooking—he is. I grew up anticipating a career, not marriage and children. My own mother had a career, which was a rarity for a married woman living in a small French town.

"If you like what you do, your child knows it, and usually accepts the situation. My older son once asked me if my company employed men as well as women because he wanted a job! There are adjustments. We're big on contingency planning. Larry and I don't waste much time on petty crises and arguments over little issues, like household chores. Some professional women trap *themselves* into traditional roles. Never assume that you'll continue just as you have all along."

The Schroeders, Ashford & Simpson, Hattie Winston and Harold Wheeler, Stephen and Fredrica Friedman, Barbara Haskell and Leon Botstein, and others you'll meet in this chapter are determined to make the most of two-career family living. Their children aren't custom-designed automatons, bursting from the womb with built-in empathy for moms and dads who take pleasure in raising career stakes along with babies. While many do have access to additional helpers, a surprising number of partners have opted to take on the bulk of child care duties themselves, at least for the first few years.

All of us hope that the corporate world will wake up and see the van in the driveway, be it a Jeep or Volvo. Even those of us who have chosen not to raise children will reap the benefits of a more humane workplace. Until that day comes, there is much that the caring two-career couple can do to develop affirmative family feelings—for their children, for other close relatives, and especially for each other. While there are no pat solutions, even Hochschild predicts in *Newsweek's* special issue on the twenty-first-century family that by the year 2020, the situation will improve. Power Partners have the tools to attempt a daring thirty-year head start; not surprisingly, most of them are succeeding.

THE GUILT GLITCH

"They're almost like thirteenth-century Catholics." That's how Pat Schroeder describes the flexibility quotient of the average school-age child. "They demand routine in their lives. That was a real surprise for me. My kids used to sit down every night and go through a litany of who was here, who was not, who did this, who wanted what."

In the same breath, the congresswoman admits that she has rarely suffered the slings and arrows of culpability over leaving her children to go to work. "I was never overpoweringly guilty. When I dropped my daughter at the day care center, she would scream her head off. A short time later, I'd call in from a phone booth and all I would hear was contented giggling. Some kids are Oscar-caliber actors, others do require more attention."

Leroy C. Richie, general counsel to Chrysler Motors, had a ruder awakening to how hard it is for even a secure youngster to accept change. "I've always made 'deals' with each of my daughters. Both know that there will usually be set blocks of time for each of them to spend time alone with me. This system was working quite well until I spent several months at home with a back injury. Suddenly, my youngest found that she had a lot more of me than she was used to—

naturally, she liked it! The trouble began when I resumed my usual work week routine."

The Richies' older daughter wrote her father a distressing letter, telling him that her little sister had lost trust in him and that he needed to talk to her. "Of course, she was really speaking for herself, too," admits Richie. "I sat them both down and told them that their time expectations were too great for our current 'deal.' I told them to help me work out a better arrangement . . . and they did. Now we have a 'new deal' that's easier for me to keep and which satisfies them; I don't feel guilty and they don't pressure me if 'the deal' occasionally doesn't work out. They know that I *want* to spend time with them. That's what we really had to establish."

Routines don't have to be traditional to provide emotional security. Curator Barbara Haskell and college president Leon Botstein have an inquisitive, lively daughter who has a strong sense of where she and her parents belong—surprising, considering that Barbara lives in Manhattan, away from the rest of the family, for several days a week. When asked where she goes to school, the girl replies, "Bard." She was quick to tell us that she meant the nursery school, not the college . . . yet.

Despite the fact that she hadn't seen her mother for several days, the preschooler wasn't overly clingy—she greeted a beaming Barbara with the same affection and intensity of any contented child who was taking part in a familiar family ritual. In this case, it was coming into town to "meet Mommy" and maybe go out for a treat. Her main concern was whether the apples on her mother's desk were ripe enough.

"Our daughter knows the difference between how we live and kids whose parents aren't together," explains Botstein. "Barbara is on the phone with her all the time, and she sees me on the phone with Barbara, too. She hears loving words and talk about family plans. Sometimes she comes into the city and spends a night with her mother. But her home is on the campus. It's really not that different than having a parent who travels. In fact, since the pattern is nearly always the same, it's less disruptive for all of us. Barbara and I spent a good deal of time sorting out how we were going to make this work. Both of us came from close families—I think that helps."

In a 1989 *Newsweek* cover story, noted child expert Dr. T. Berry Brazelton emphasized that working parents who feel guilty about leaving their children in the morning are usually more likely to work out satisfying solutions. Brazelton's philosophies about parent-child interactions are based on the presumption that the two-career family is definitely here to stay. He stresses that while the first few months of infancy are critical times for both mothers and fathers, older babies and children do not necessarily have to suffer if parents choose to keep their careers in relatively high gear. And, like Pat Schroeder, with whom he has lobbied for working parents, he believes that the "supermom" with her "superbaby" is an unhealthy mythology that can only lead to more bad feelings on everyone's part.

SMART PARENTS, MANY CHOICES

When working women like book editor Fredrica Friedman and investment banking consultant Myrna Weiss were in the initial throes of child-rearing, they had few doubts about who or what came first. "Stephen and I have taken turns. When the kids were little, he was the one who commuted from Washington, D.C.," Fredrica says.

"Fredi was a working mother," says Stephen. "She plateaued, but fortunately she was also able to make fast-track contacts in her less intensive position at that time. I'd say that was a miracle."

Recalls Fredrica, "Steve was the primary earner. For me, marriage has always been an infinite set of accommodations. You must each allocate responsibility. My children were more important than my career. I knew that later on, when they were in college, I could get in gear again . . .

which I did. You can't always predict life perfectly, but with children, you only get one chance."

Myrna Weiss, who is married to an eminent neurologist, feels that her own adult daughter has fewer *personal* options "because there are so many professional paths." She looks back at her early married life. "I was the breadwinner when Arthur was getting started. At that time, I was a school headmistress."

Weiss continued to expand her career horizons and build her family life. "I had good help at home and 'spaced' children. Even when I traveled, I could make most trips in a day—I made sure that they were kept short. And I had a supportive husband in Arthur."

She believes, however, that she was freer to balance her two lives as she saw suitable. "I could move ahead as much as I wanted . . . or not. Women today are more constrained. Working mothers coming up today must ask themselves if they really want to remain in the corporate world—and why. Spouses have to decide who will give more care . . . where they should live . . . how much money they need. If the couple can come to terms with those variables, it can work. Many people don't perceive these decisions as *choices*; I've seen hard-driving career women disappear into the Connecticut woods with their horses and children. For them, it's one or the other kind of lifestyle."

But many women under forty-five aren't disappearing or suffering from confusion about their current work/child-rearing status. They tend to see their family life flowing directly from their marital partnerships.

Sara, a Cleveland-area child psychiatrist, admits that she enjoys carrying the bulk of the "second shift." "Women, more than men, have to make a decision as to what will make them happy. A child should have contented parents whether they're home or at work. All of us worry that we're not around enough. My husband is a lawyer. He puts in long hours. I know that if I were a surgeon or an anesthesiologist, raising my child would be tougher. Personally, I would probably cut back or rethink my career in favor of spending more time with my baby."

She admits that she and her husband are relatively old-fashioned when it comes to organizing their household. "I love taking care of my husband and child. I'm proud of my practice and I know that much of my identity is tied up with my work. But there are certain times when nothing comes ahead of my family. This is just the way I am. Other couples have different attitudes."

Valerie Simpson thinks that she and husband Nick Ashford are giving their kids substantial "wings" by not trying to twist themselves into what, for them, would be uncomfortable traditional roles. "We want our kids to see our life as *natural*," says Valerie. "I feel that our older daughter understands that the way I live gives us this special lifestyle. I'm not crazy about being an 'earth mother.' "

Adds Nick, "I think that you can spend too much time with a child. The way you *act* when you are with them is important. That's how they learn values. I don't think that parents should be afraid of encouraging their child to engage in parentless play. I like seeing our daughters go off to their rooms and talk to their dolls and stuffed animals. They won't become as creative or resourceful if you're always around to organize their lives."

Valerie says, "We don't shield our older daughter from the bumps and down sides of our life, like weirdo fans and work pressures. Nick and I talk about showing her the less prosperous, more realistic neighborhoods. That's New York. I don't want her to be crippled."

Barbara Lamont admits that she spent a good deal of time away from her children while they were growing up. "I was living in Lagos, Nigeria. My husband took over most of the routine parenting."

She and Ludwig Gelobter admit that their unorthodox approach to family life has had some effect on their oldest son. Barbara recalls how he casually announced, "You and Dad are real screw-ups."

"I think he felt that we didn't give him enough security

when he was young. We were always moving around and changing careers," admits Barbara. "There wasn't much concern over locking up savings in a bank or establishing set routines."

Gelobter points out that their oldest child has also had a more difficult time coming to grips with his mixed racial heritage. "No one can understand what it's like being black unless you are. I think he also resented having to be the 'big brother' to his younger siblings. Many first children go through that. At the same time, I think we've given our children a great feeling of openness. We've worked hard to keep them away from stereotypical concepts. Barbara and I want them to feel that they can do whatever they want—success is not a function of race, sex, or class. It's what you want from life."

Both Ludwig and Barbara believe that, despite some problems, their three children have benefited by their various professional changes. "Kids learn from you from the moment they're born," observes Barbara. "We've had some bad moments, but Ludwig and I have achieved more than we've failed. And we've stayed married and in love with each other, too!"

Ludwig concurs. "Our oldest son had to leave college and spend a year working on a show horse farm before he was ready to resume his education. Now he's getting his doctorate. While Barbara and I both think that education is extremely important, the fact that we've both been through so many changes ourselves helped us to see his point of view. We're pleased that all of them are strong and independent. We've given them the ability to be comfortable in any surroundings. I think that's all to the good these days."

Leroy and Julia Richie have always put family values first. "The irony is," says Julia, "that what started out as decisions based around our daughters' well-being has increased our ability to function as a couple."

Julia, who has worked for such major corporations as Arthur Andersen and AT&T, recently decided to quit the executive fast track in order to free up her time. As it's turning out, Julia Richie is almost as busy with the National League of Women Voters, the Birmingham, Michigan, Board of Zoning Appeals, and her participation on several corporate boards. "But there is a vast difference in the way I *feel*," she explains. "I'm more flexible in terms of setting my own work schedules. Even with high-level volunteerism, you can say no if you want to stay home with your child or meet your husband for a long weekend. Roy teases me about being so intense—but I know that I'm much more relaxed inside. My children can sense the difference. This is what I need in my life right now. Later, I may choose another path."

Carol Colman's ambition was to become a successful nonfiction author. Until the birth of her son, she was the on-air public affairs director for a New York radio station. "I had already won most of the major broadcast journalism awards before my thirtieth birthday," Carol recalls. "My husband had made the switch from corporate to academic law. We were settled in terms of where we wanted to live. In terms of starting a family, we couldn't have been in a much better position."

After the baby's birth, Carol made her move. "I had already published one or two books without much fanfare. Now that I am devoting all of my work energies toward writing and working with my agent, both the advances and the sales have picked up enormously. My son is amazingly attuned to what I do. While I have some daytime help, my husband and I are really the primary care-givers. His schedule, though packed, is less grueling than it would be if he worked in a firm. In a way, having a child has led us toward where *we* want to be in terms of our careers. And I think that when our child starts school in a year or so, he'll be much more enthusiastic about his own work."

Like Julia Richie, Carol gladly accepts any difficulties that come with not having a title before her name. "Knowing that when my child has intersession, I can also 'take off' time is definitely worth it. When our son is older, some of that flexibility will be put to good use for myself. In fact, if it weren't for what I was doing now, I wouldn't be able to help my own parents with their chores, or even sneak in an indulgent afternoon's shopping trip.''

All of these mothers and fathers have their good and bad days . . . as professionals and as parents. What's different is that they *accept* the challenge without the expectation of perfection. None of the mothers here would consider themselves compromised because they've made their career-change decisions for themselves.

"Mommy Track is awful," says Pat Schroeder. "It's back to the superwoman issue. You end up losing it all, and no one gets wings in the process."

Amy Binder, president of Ruder & Finn's public relations New York office, agrees. "I don't believe in that concept at all. When I was pregnant with my first child [she and her physician husband have two boys and a girl], I really resented people who asked me if I was going to work full-time after the baby arrived. My kids are well adjusted. Sure, we have to make extra efforts at providing family time together, but that's a joy. Once in a while, they'll complain about my not being around enough during the week. But when I'm there all weekend, they'll go off by themselves and play. They're happy just knowing that I'm in the house. To me, that's a sign of security."

Binder stresses that it's how children *feel* when you and your spouse are not around that counts. "My kids know that they come first. My secretary always finds me when one of them calls. The other night, I didn't get home until after ten, but I made sure to stop off and bring the boys the Nerf candies they had called me about earlier in the day."

Donna Karan and Stephan Weiss are another set of partners who have their priorities in the right place. Says Karan, "Family is the balance in our life. Living just for your profession doesn't work. I knew this early in my career. You can't compare family to a business—the family is here forever, while associates move through your life. For Stephan and myself, business is the means and family is the end. The ultimate creation is your children."

Forging New Family Alliances

Working parents are changing the face of the family dinner hour. Letitia Baldrige believes that children should be treated as equals when it comes to holding court at the evening meal. "Parents have to give more than 'quality time.' Couples should include kids in their social life—if time is tight, they should come before friends. Children should take pride at being a family member. Spouses ought to adopt each other's heritage. I'm a great supporter of taking out old photographs and letting younger generations learn about their ancestors. I display pictures of my husband's relatives all over our home."

At the Richies' house in a Detroit suburb, each family member takes turns "hosting" the evening meal. Leroy explains, "The host sits at the head of the table. He or she is responsible for initiating the topics of discussion. This is great for everyone, especially our younger daughter. Even our housekeeper takes part."

Adds Julia, "We also use this as a time when the girls can share in Roy's day and he in theirs. Sometimes I have to do a bit of 'translating.' I might say, 'This is a good time to ask Daddy about that assignment you got.' Roy doesn't always share that easily. I become an interpreter."

Both Richies work hard to instill their children with a sense of responsibility. "Our daughters must learn that relationships are built on trust and work. Roy and I don't hide much from them when it comes to talking about finances or plans for the future. They see us argue and make up. The girls know that we function as a family even though we all have our own agendas, too."

Jim Cusick thinks that his and Gail Blanke's two children have benefited by their ambitious streaks. "Because we're both pursuing careers, we've grown as people. With both of us working, the kids see more compromise. The housekeeper shops, I do all the cooking. Sometimes I disappear deep into a particular project, and Gail takes on the bulk of the homemaking. It keeps changing. Our children tend to be independent—they have to be. I don't think that it's bad for them to reach into their inner selves. Our older daughter is particularly self-motivated. We've taken both of them on many trips. We're close, but not smothering."

Gail agrees with her husband's outlook. "Children want to be respected. We want them to feel good about themselves, and to know that they are loved. Our children aren't shut out of Jim's and my professional lives. When Jim went to Tokyo, he sat down and explained what he was doing there. He brought back an abacus and other unusual items. Sometimes, I'm jealous of Jim when he gets to spend more time with them. Men have been in that position of being the more 'absent' parent all of their lives. I do admit that balancing my time and priorities was easier with the second than the first. But I've always believed that I was *good* enough to get to the top and raise children who wouldn't feel deprived."

Dr. Brazelton also believes in the importance of a family dinner hour. In his writings, he emphasizes that too many parents of small children concentrate too much on adequate food consumption when they should be paying attention to socializing. "Your relationship is more important. If a child won't eat vegetables, give her a multivitamin every day. Don't make food an issue."

Of course, some two-career households can't stage a Waltons-style mealtime scene every weekday evening; and older children schedule occasional evening activities. But just as Power Partners know the importance of taking time out for each other, they quickly realize that when it comes to satisfying family life, there's no substitute for relaxed, ongoing interaction. Even Vice President Dan Quayle and his wife, Marilyn, keep several nights free each week for family-style dining. But if establishing a regular dinner hour is difficult, try one of the following tactics:

- Just as Leroy Richie has done, negotiate individual time "deals" with each child and adolescent. Be sure to give advance warning if you cannot meet your end of the bargain because of travel or other work commitments. Most children are surprisingly forgiving if you take an honest approach. Be sure to make up the special time alone as soon as possible. That way, trust won't be broken.

• Keep weekends available for family plans. This doesn't mean that you cannot allot yourself any private time together, or enjoy your friends' company. What it does mean is that your children's time needs come *first*. Many professional couples now plan entertaining around the needs of their brethren; party menus often include recipes that can be easily adapted for younger palates. "Bring the kids" is fast becoming the byword in many affluent and sophisticated communities. If children aren't included in the invitation, it won't hurt to explain to your host why you both must decline.

• Take children along on *your* favorite leisure activities. In New York, Los Angeles, and Chicago, you'll find dozens of wide-eyed infants and curious toddlers milling around major museums and other "adult" locales. Even elegant restaurants loosen up for Sunday brunch. Unless your child is unusually cranky or unruly, no one will try and stanch her enthusiasm. You may even learn something new about art or music by watching your son's or daughter's responses. As Linda McCartney has said of her four offspring, "I find them much more interesting than many of the so-called interesting people I meet." In her recently published cookbook, she spends several pages discussing ways of getting both children and husbands involved in daily meal preparation and planning.

• Take a class or learn a new skill together. Harriet Craig Peterson, vice president of marketing for the Radisson Hotel Corporation, took a jazz aerobics class with her eleven-year-old daughter. "I can't tell you how much fun we had planning our recital. We both gained new confidence, and took pride in each other's efforts. It opened up a new avenue of communication. When time is at a premium, it's so important not to waste it on the trivial."

How you and your mate treat your time together is a good barometer for measuring the way that you regard time spent with your children. Couples whose needs are being met are more likely to meet their children's needs without undue pressure. The more you and your spouse increase your co-mentoring abilities, the more relaxed and flexible your family life should become. No matter what any article (or book) may recommend, the best system is the one that *works* . . . for all of you!

PRIVATE CHILDREN, PUBLIC PARENTS

In chapter 3, we examined the pressures public couples face at the hands of a demanding outside world. Children of recognized parents face special problems, most of which stem from situations outside the family unit. If a parent is sensitive from the start, there's no reason to fear that your or your spouse's visibility will incur any serious emotional side effects. Psychologist Evelyn Sherburne agrees.

"I treat a broad range of families, many of them lower-income. Their kids tend to suffer similar degree of stress as more affluent children of well-known people. Again, it's a question of the parents putting their children's needs first at the right moments. Splitting up, no matter who you are, can cause trouble. Also, some of those mothers and fathers have unrealistic expectations of their children—but so do factory foremen and accountants!"

Hattie Winston and Harold Wheeler are parents who are well aware of how children of entertainers and artists can find themselves in difficult situations outside the home.

"We're extremely involved in our daughter's education," says Hattie. "We check up often to make sure that she isn't being pushed into areas like music and drama because teachers 'expect' it of her. For instance, at the moment, she's much more interested in stage managing than in acting; we want her to be able to develop those skills without pressure."

Harold remembers when their daughter started piano lessons. "Normally, a parent is supposed to come to every third lesson and observe. Her teacher recognized me. I won't interfere. On the other hand, I expect them to teach her without feeling intimidated. When she practices at home, I sometimes allow her to make mistakes without correcting them—that's the piano teacher's job."

Nick Ashford and Valerie Simpson are giving their older daughter piano lessons, too. "But it's for the discipline and practice," explains Valerie. "If she wants to take up something else, that's fine with us."

Performers and other public professionals must also make certain that their kids have a clear picture of reality. When Mom makes a speech on TV or Dad shoots the good guy in the movie, the child must be made aware that this is simply a part of the job, no more or less than readying an annual report or performing surgery in an operating room.

"Our daughter knows what's real and make-believe," says Hattie Winston. "She's seen me cry in front of the camera. When I played the part of an abusive aunt to a little boy on a PBS special, I carefully explained that this was a show."

In contrast, both Hattie and Harold make sure that their child knows when a harmful word or situation is real. "There have been times when she's heard me rehearse and someone uses a racial slur," Hattie explains. "But my daughter has also been taught that sometimes people use bad words or do wrong in real life, and that she must never confuse the two. I think that children learn through actions—parents must always be as clear and honest as possible when it comes to communicating with a child."

Odd Kid on the Block

Other trouble areas for children of achievers, especially those in the public eye, are living up to expectations—the community's and their parents'—and sustaining the comforting feeling of "being like everyone else." Over the past several years, we've read about dubious means of raising "brighter" children. Some "experts" even claim that aggressive parents should read books and play classical music to their unborn child. And as soon as the infant leaves the womb, he or she should instantly be enrolled in everything from violin lessons to aerobics class.

While two-career couples can provide a more intellectually stimulating home environment, the benefits to the child should come from increased opportunities for participation and nonsexist exposure to learning situations. If a school-age boy sees his mother cooking and then hears her talk about designing a new housing development, chances are he'll come to Mommy for chocolate chip cookies *and* help with his Lego constructions. Similarly, a young girl whose father teaches creative writing at the local college will turn to Daddy for a really great bedtime story. If Daddy also pitches in with the weekly laundry and supermarket shopping, so much the better!

"People tell my daughter how she never saw me in the kitchen, right?" Pat Schroeder laughs. "She chuckles and tells them that I really did do a lot of the cooking."

Adds Jim Schroeder, "In a two-career household, you get a real partnership. Shared concerns—the kids, school, health problems, the house. People take equal responsibility. The kids see that one parent alone cannot do everything. As they get older, kids see this as a joint effort. In our home, they may see me doing the wash and then ask Pat for the car keys or extra spending money."

He also believes that dynamic, "spotlight" households must make an extra effort to take on some of life's more mundane chores for themselves, or children will get an undesirable impression of how life really operates. "Some families give outsiders all the responsibility. No one does anything personally for family life. The whole scene collapses."

Sustaining a sense of normalcy is crucial for establishing values and a sense of self-worth. In a recent *Parade* magazine article, actress Jamie Lee Curtis talked about how hard her mother, Janet Leigh, worked to give her and her sister as "normal" a childhood as possible.

"We lived on a dirt road up Benedict Canyon. I was a typical California little girl, running around in shorts and tennis shoes, swimming and making tree forts."

In the same piece, Janet Leigh described how Jamie wore her sister's hand-me-downs. "I wasn't going to deny that we had money, because that's what you work for. But I did try to maintain a balance. I wanted her to learn that just because her mom and dad were in a profession that had this celebrity didn't mean we had any different standards or beliefs than anyone else."

The McCartneys' solution was to move themselves from London to a more rural environment. Paul's children have all attended state schools. "There is a rationale behind trying to live in a village community—not to spoil them," he told a British newspaper. "We go to school meetings in the town hall as parents, not as speakers or celebrities. I won't open bazaars or anything, because it means all the other parents perceive me as a big star."

In an interview with the *Washington Post*, Marilyn Quayle discussed her own way of retaining the flavor of her pre-vice-presidential life. She confessed that some of her favorite private moments are when she carpools her kids and their friends.

"I had a van, and I would pile everybody in, and I'd take the soccer teams, I'd take everyone everywhere. But I knew everything that was going on. I'd sit there quiet as a little mouse, listening to their conversations, and you'd know what's going on in your children's lives."

She admits that carpooling has changed a bit since her move to Washington. "I took four kids to camp (last summer) and all their gear, and we'll do the carpool for school dances. It's kind of odd because I'm sitting back with the kids."

Even Diana, the Princess of Wales, drives her two boys to school and gives them their nightly baths whenever possible. And our own working "royal," Jacqueline Onassis, managed to raise her son and daughter away from most prying lenses while developing her own successful career as a book editor. Caroline Kennedy Schlossberg appears to be following the same route with child-rearing.

"Interacting is enormously important," comments Dr. Ann Curtain Ward. "Encourage kids to participate in your lives and share in household routines. I see many children from achieving homes who are skilled in baking, sewing, and other practical areas. I'm all for that. Children need to see that running a home is a mutual effort in which everyone should participate."

As children grow up, others around them in the community may single them out because of one or both parents' professions. Pat Schroeder recalls how wonderful it was when she and her family moved to Washington, D.C. "In Denver, they were like the preacher's children," she says. "A classmate might come up and say, 'My dad says your mom did such-and-such.' In Washington, they were just another set of congressional kids. It was easy for them to fade into the background and have their own lives."

"Parents who are in the public eye must take the time to help their children and teens work out any feelings of resentment and insecurity," Dr. Ward cautions. "In my practice, I usually find that the parents who are most secure with their own achievement find it easy to relate to their kids."

When sons and daughters reach adolescence, problems with self-worth can arise in conjunction with dating and other social activities. It's one thing if the teenager's environment is filled with individuals like himself or herself—quite another if they're the only superstar offspring in town. A sportswear designer who is married to a familiar face on national TV remembers the agonies of her oldest son's early courtships.

"It wasn't the girls—they got crushes for the right reasons. My son was on the football and debate teams. When you're six foot two without pimples at sixteen, what your folks do means nothing . . . except to gold-digging parents. I remember one mother who practically offered up her daughter in marriage. My son dated the girl for a few months and then, like all kids at that age, moved on. You should have heard some of the phone calls we got. Even the father begged us to try and get them back together. These people weren't poor or without community standing. The whole incident made our boy suspicious for quite some time. It wasn't until he went off to college that he finally shrugged off those times."

GREAT EXPECTATIONS

Children and teens need to feel loved and respected as unique individuals—not as reflections of their parents' glories. Often, as we've demonstrated, the problem lies with the adults in their lives. Teachers, religious and civic community leaders, and other authority figures place unrealistic expectations on the sons and daughters of the uncommonly successful. Hattie Winston and Harold Wheeler are keeping a watchful eye on their child's schooling to make certain that her own talents, rather than her parents', are nurtured; it's equally vital for the child of a bond trader or product development manager to experience the same freedom from slotting.

If one or more of your children do begin taking an interest in your or your spouse's career, it's fine to feel proud—just don't push. Power Partners have learned the pitfalls of intramarital competition. Competing with your child can leave lifetime scars. And never set your children up for failure at anything they may attempt to undertake. Telling a youngster who's having trouble with algebra that "I never got the hang of binomials either" can be extremely comforting. But watch out for phrases like "At your age, I was acing calculus," or "Your father flunked math and got left back." Words like these not only discourage, but erode good feelings of family teamwork.

Successful couples often feel that they are entitled to successful children. One female lawyer, married to a national housewares retailer, actually began harboring resentment toward her toddler son when he didn't make the cut at a prestigious nursery school. Fortunately, she and her husband talked out their anxieties in time.

"Here we were with this gorgeous, articulate, coordinated little bundle who had never let us down at anything. He toilet-trained himself in record time. He knew our home phone number at age three. When he was rejected by this selective school, I felt humiliated. Suddenly, I had fantasies of him being bullied in the sandbox, not making valedictorian, failing to get into Wharton. As it turned out, the main reason that he didn't get accepted was simply his age. The school had recently started an arbitrary policy of not enrolling kids who hadn't reached four by the previous summer.

"This was a scary moment for me," she confesses. "My husband had worked hard to come up through the ranks in public schools and colleges. I was the first woman in my family to attend an Ivy League university. It actually took me a day to realize that what happened was no reflection on my kid's intelligence . . . or ours. He's now enrolled in a delightful playschool where the parents are as terrific as the children. They do a lot more than the place that wouldn't take him. I never realized how much of my identity is caught up in my son. Being a parent is a hell of a lot trickier than trying a case. There's no one set of laws or rules to follow."

Amy Binder and her spouse found themselves falling into a similar trap. "When we started to look for grade schools, I began to think more about status and college admissions than about my kids' feelings. Fortunately, as I toured one of the toughest New York private schools, I began to think about all those horrible pressures which they would be facing each day. We opted for a high-quality but less-aggressive school. Now I care about the important aspects of their education—like fostering creativity and independence. I see many of my friends going through the same sort of experience. They overstuff their kids' days with 'enrichment.' We've made an effort to cut back and just let them be kids."

Dr. Ward warns about another psychological red flag that could trigger trouble for the child of highly visible parents. "Sometimes you get a man or woman who makes child-rearing decisions based on his or her public image. These individuals can't relate to their families as private human beings. That's extremely damaging for the kids. No matter who you are, once you're with your family, you must relate as a husband, wife, and parent."

She continues. "Some image-conscious parents even go so far as to relocate the child—they force the boy or girl to leave *their* domain if he or she can't measure up. Other mothers and fathers go overboard in the opposite direction. These couples 'overrepresent' the child to their colleagues, creating an impossible set of expectations."

POWERFUL PARENTING: PLANNING, PRIORITIES, AND PARTNERSHIP

In a survey of new mothers and fathers conducted by *Parenting* magazine, first-time parents who viewed themselves as partners rather than romantic lovers had an easier adjustment to family living.

Which doesn't mean that your children should be the *only* focus of your life before and after work. You and your spouse must work out a set of home-life priorities that provide relatively smooth emotional sailing for everyone. As with other aspects of your marriage, prepare for surprises— both accommodating and bothersome. Lack of anticipation is often the hardest hurdle. You and your spouse must work together and look to the future. Your children will forgive your mistakes (as you must forgive theirs) if you take steps to work the problem out the next time around.

Here is some advice for parents who love their children and their careers:

1. Take time to give each child a sense of individual importance within the family. Like the Richies, develop a routine together and stick to it as much as

possible. Most child care authorities agree that emotionally healthy children don't need more than several hours each week of such communication—but make the commitment to give them that time.

2. Show your children where you work and encourage them to ask questions about what you do. Once a young child sees that Mommy and Daddy are really *doing* something when they're not around, he'll be less resentful of your separations. Even toddlers enjoy looking at computer screens and colorful wall charts. When you work at home, let the child "help" by keeping track of paper clips or, if she's old enough, filing, sorting, and even brainstorming. Encourage kids to do their own homework by inviting them to sit with you while you go through your next day's planning.

3. Stay in touch. Dr. Ward says that media executives are among the most resourceful working parents because they're not afraid to take advantage of high-tech helpers like fax machines and car phones. "I know one woman who was right in the thick of the Malta summit, but she still managed to call her children every morning. If you or your spouse have to miss the school play, tape it or, better yet, set time aside for your child to act out her role at home . . . recording her solo performance. And remember, you can still help with homework while you're stuck in traffic."

4. Don't be lax about setting limits. When one parent travels, the other must be firm about rules and restrictions. Sometimes the home spouse feels angry about having total responsibility, or guilty about the child's temporary deprivation of a mother or father. This can result in slippage of constructive discipline and boundaries. "A child must not be allowed to feel that he or she can behave differently than if both parents were present," says Dr. Ward. "I have to teach fathers, especially, the importance

of maintaining the status quo when it comes to snacks, sleeping away from home, and staying out late."

5. Develop a network of two-career families. No matter where you live, you and your mate are *not* alone! Share information and angst with each other. Form associations and work as a group to improve situations at work and at home. Encourage your children to play together. As discussed earlier, kids long to feel that secure sense of "sameness." If you've recently moved because of a career change, make an effort to join the local PTA and other parents' groups. Many large cities also have organizations designed specifically to help working mothers.

6. Harness career skills to your child-rearing efforts. Just as you and your partner organize chores by ability rather than gender, the two of you can apply the identical principle to organizing most aspects of child care. If you're impatient and nervous about bathtime, let your mate take over. Even better, get your feet (and everything else) wet together. Carry this attitude over into more complex emotional areas like discipline, sex education, and personal ethics. It doesn't matter who takes the lead; what's critical is that these areas aren't neglected.

   Many two-career families have a part-time or full-time outside care-giver. This can be of enormous benefit to all of you if the helper is properly trained and genuinely enthusiastic about spending time with your child. U.S. special trade representative (and former cabinet secretary) Carla Hills has pointed out that "a lot of women spend more time interviewing their secretaries than they do their care-givers. Your children are your most precious assets, so the person you should hire should be the best you can find."

7. Get help. If you and your children are coping, don't worry if your lifestyle doesn't mirror that of Bill

Cosby's Huxtables. But when tensions begin to get the better of you, or if you suspect that one or more of your progeny are not as contented or productive as usual, don't be afraid to consult with a qualified counselor, psychologist, or psychiatrist. "There's no stigma in seeking help," affirms Dr. Ward. "If you had a problem with your business, you would call in an expert before the situation got out of hand. If you and your spouse came to an impasse, you would do the same. Why not with your children?"

Dr. Ward emphasizes that in many cases, therapies are usually short-term and surprisingly targeted. "No one is suggesting that a young child lie on a couch for the next five years. But the right therapist can do wonders for parents and children who are starting to hurt. I frequently find myself in the role of a constructive catalyst who helps to put everyone back on track. Being a working mother myself, I know the sorts of problems that can crop up all too easily."

8. Open new doors. You and your spouse are well on the way toward realizing your ambitions. Give your children and teens the exciting opportunity of discovering what *they* wish to achieve. "A mother (or father) who is adept at presenting herself—someone like a Christie Brinkley or a Paul Newman—tends to develop their child's natural talents instead of pushing their own to the fore," says Dr. Ward. If an older child expresses interest in pursuing your line of work, give them an accurate picture. Help set up a summer job in a similar type of company—but not your own.

"A little competitiveness isn't necessarily bad," says Dr. Ward. "Kirk and Michael Douglas are a good example of a father and son who have extremely different approaches to the same career. What parents have to accept is that while they may find the emulation flattering, their sons and daughters will most likely not do it 'their way.' " As with other problems, you and your children should talk out the tensions that can arise when the younger generation succeeds sooner than expected.

9. Recognize your own deficits. Don't try and compensate for them in your kids. If your son hates football, accept the fact that he'll never make the touchdown you missed twenty years ago. When your daughter tells you that she'd rather take honors chemistry than drama, don't weep over your lost Juliet. Children are people with lives and drives of their own. Enjoy their strengths and accept their shortcomings—you'll be pleasantly surprised at how easily they'll return the favor. As one grown executive daughter remarked, "My mom was never a contender for bake-sale blue ribbons, but thanks to her knack with a hammer and saw, I had the coolest tree house in the neighborhood—and I didn't have all that baby fat to lose!"

10. Make family living a *mutual arrangement*. Let your co-mentoring attitudes permeate your relationship with your children. Transfer your good feelings for each other to everyone else who lives under your roof. Encourage independence while offering security. Don't sacrifice—look for solutions that give all concerned at least a partial win. Women must permit their husbands to do more.

"No man is going to take over if they're uncomfortable," says Pat Schroeder. "We have to be mindful of how our actions are perceived. We tend to act as if we know more about child care. That's *our* big mistake. No one enjoys feeling like a beginner. We bitch that men don't do enough, but guess who's setting them up?"

THERE'S STILL NO PLACE LIKE HOME

Today's Dorothys and their spouses usually ask the Wizard for brains, heart, and courage—and do they ever need them! But no one can afford to ignore the strength derived from growing up together in a dynamic and loving home environment. We should all strive to create such a place for ourselves and our children. The concept of that home has changed radically since the days of June Cleaver and Jim Anderson. Father and Mother don't always know best. Dad may be seasoning as well as carving the roast while Mom is struggling with the last shuttle flight. There may be additional care-givers in the picture. The house that shelters the home may change with each passing promotion. Under its roof, everyone appears in a constant state of motion.

Which is why partnering two-career parents and their children can thrive. Standing still holds us back, as does throwing away the past. Couples who manage to maintain traditional bonds of love and commitment while exploring new personal and professional horizons will make the most successful parents.

When both parents work, the home becomes a more potentially exciting and enriching place. When couples share their workday lives, stimulation doesn't stop with the school bell or the click of the VCR. Ideas for solving problems at home and in the office can come from the quick mind of a resourceful nine-year-old. Ideally, this is a haven where everyone works, loves, and sometimes struggles together.

The next century will not, as some doomsayers like to speculate, be the end of the line for the family or the nuclear home. Just as our bodies have adapted to environmental changes in the atmosphere, so couples and their children will find new ways to express familial unity. As with our environment, we must preserve as well as forge ahead. Love, respect, concern, and dignity must always be in the mix, as should commitment and communication. After that, it's up to each family to find its own best path to follow. As you've seen in this chapter, there are no fixed solutions to the dilemmas of raising children in two-career homes. But that isn't stopping anyone here. Where there's a willing partner, there's always a way.

6

SIDE-BY-SIDE STRATEGIES

♦

Co-preneuring is the ultimate Power Partnership—the two of you working and profiting together in your very own business. Each picks and chooses what he or she enjoys doing best. No more guilt about leaving the children— running the show provides unlimited flextime. An end to wasted energy psyching out difficult supervisors and co-workers. You can bed the boss and no one gives a hoot . . . including your own spouse. Finally, here is an approach to dual-career marriage that answers everyone's needs and prayers.

If you took the previous paragraph at face value, you've been reading this book upside down. Serious students of co-mentoring know there's no such luck or escape from com-mitment, conflicts, decision-making, and the potential for problems. None of which has stopped the couples in this chapter from running successful businesses while enriching the personal aspects of their marriages.

Couples who choose to co-preneur and usually succeed are Power Partners *first*, business partners *second*. They've spent months, and in some cases years, developing the sup-portive skills needed to help each other achieve in the workplace. These are men and women who know each other's blind spots and pressure points. They are not fleeing from painful dismissals or bounding headlong into fantasies of island-hopping weekends and limitless tax deductions. Their ventures work because they develop naturally out of a shared passion, such as cooking or designing furniture. Or it may be a shared goal that's more easily reached by merging two careers into a single income-generating family business. Or it may be that both spouses realize that one spouse's involvement can provide the crucial breakthrough a company needs.

And, yet, not even that may be enough to keep most of these ambitious pairs working and loving together for the duration. The fact is that the majority of co-preneurs end up winning the business laurels and losing the rest of their relationships.

Doug and Sue Tompkins of Esprit sportswear built an empire together and are now in the midst of an "amicable" separation of their enormous assets and themselves. On a less lofty level, the Nelsons, a Texas couple who owned a successful hardware delivery company, broke up over the long hours that came with expansion. Jerry Nelson told the *Wall Street Journal* that he decided to close part of the business because the divorce was too distracting.

Plainly, the rules of Power Partnering that we've described and illustrated by themselves aren't the only ingredients in the recipe. Some mysterious alchemy, as well as a commitment to the Power Partner lifestyle, is at work in those truly successful and *enduring* co-preneurial marriages. In this chapter, we'll meet a number of pairs who have, thus far, mastered the intricacies of the mix. Their words provide eloquent inspiration and direction for those who wish to try their own four hands and two hearts.

PAIRS WHO'VE PROFITED

Jeff and Jacky Clyman are the founders of Avirex, the leather fashion company that provided bomber jackets for the movie *The Right Stuff* and was involved in the promotion of *Top Gun*. They also run boutiques, appropriately named Cockpit, in New York and Los Angeles, and have recently negotiated to open branches at major American airports. Including licenses and worldwide distribution, their company is valued at around $200 million. Jeff holds a law degree and Jacky has done interpreting for the State Department in Washington, D.C. They live in Manhattan, where they are raising their two children.

Jacky laughs when asked how they got into this highly specialized end of the "rag trade."

"Jeff was working for his uncle," she recalls. "He had gotten tired of law, so we moved from D.C. to New York. Jeff's uncle had a real estate company. But Jeff was devoting most of his work efforts to gathering and selling World War I and II memorabilia in order to fund his personal passion—reconstructing and flying small planes."

Jeff, an intense and amiable Robert Redford lookalike, had always had a flair for design. "I have strong opinions about how clothes should look, even if I can't actually draw or create them," he says. "We started a mail order business after my uncle told me to 'get lost and go for it.' We sold old stuff. Soon, department stores started to ask for merchandise. This was in the late 1970s."

In 1979, the pair met Frank Marchese, now their partner in the venture. Explains Jeff, "He showed us the fashion potential for the old, traditional styles. We take what's real, like leather flight jackets and nylon jumpsuits, and present it as streetwear."

Jacky got involved when Jeff found that the business was growing faster than anticipated. "I said, Jacky—help! I need your administrative skills."

"I've wanted to be in business since I was a child," she says. "When I lived in Morocco I was the kid who was always selling things."

Sybil and Roger Ferguson are the founders of Diet Center, which was sold in 1988 to the Boston firm of Thomas H. Lee for $160 million.

The Fergusons, a hardworking couple who divide their time between homes in Idaho and Arizona, began their multi-million-dollar weight loss franchise operation after Sybil successfully lost sixty pounds and decided to help her friends lose weight too.

"I started to learn about nutrition and psychological reinforcement simply by going to the local library," she explains. "Then I began to enlist the help of my own doctor. In fact, even today, we advise all clients to work with their personal physicians. My doctor told me that I was at the point where I should go professional."

Roger recalls how he joined his wife in her budding career. "I was in the construction business, and then switched over to sales. I wasn't terribly happy; I knew that I could be earning more money and getting more satisfaction from work. I told Sybil, 'I can sell the way you make people feel.' "

Chimes in Sybil, "We worked together at home. We tried to identify certain areas of responsibility that didn't overlap, so that each of us would have enough to do."

"And," adds Roger, "we made certain that we had enough money set aside so that we could give our early franchisees complete financial confidence in the business."

Today, Diet Center, in which the Fergusons still own a 30 percent interest, has over 2,400 franchises across the United States and promotes its sensible approach to healthy eating with sophisticated TV commercials featuring Susan St. James.

Neither the Clymans nor the Fergusons consciously intended to become co-preneurs. But in both cases, when the chance to take the risk arose, each couple had the right frame of mind and heart. They were already confident that whatever happened to their fledgling enterprises, the end results would not be personally devastating.

"You have to be aware of the opportunity," explains Jeff Clyman. "The same applies to marriage. You have to be tuned into your relationship and also be lucky enough to have a partner who can pick up on problems. One of you has to possess those antennae—the other must be willing to listen and create something positive from the criticism."

Jacky agrees. "At least one partner must be the type who keeps questioning the relationship, and looks for signs of trouble. It's too easy to go along and ignore danger signals. There have been times when work stress has started to interfere with our marriage. I've confronted Jeff instead of pretending that everything was fine."

Jeff advises, "In business and marriage, you've got to occasionally raise the red flag."

Ted and Joyce Rice were a Kansas City couple who were looking for a way to become financially comfortable beach bums. "We loved sailing so much," says Joyce, "that we began to think about starting our own business as a way to spend more time on our boat."

The pair began to think about producing a product that could be sold at regional county fairs and art shows in the Midwest. The result was T. J. Cinnamons, whose franchised bakery products are sold in numerous gourmet and department stores across the United States. President Bush is a fan; when he was campaigning in Kansas City, his secret service agents kept coming back to the Rices' mobile unit for more. The company's estimated 1989 gross was $50 million; there are over 240 franchises.

"I wanted an alternative to teaching school," remembers Joyce. "I enjoy being with kids, but it was time to move on. I thought that Ted could take an early retirement."

Ted feels that their relatively quick success was due to hard work, creativity, and their joint enthusiasm. "We didn't have a model," Ted recollects. "I learned about putting together a mobile bakery unit bit by bit. I was an engineer, so I guess I had the knack for putting technical equipment together. Joyce came up with the cinnamon roll recipe, and no one else was making them. Our customers can actually watch the rolls baking—it's a process product. And there's that wonderful aroma. We figured that we would work about twenty weeks a year and spend the rest of the time sailing."

Soon, the Rices were on a professional roll of their own.

"We had to decide who would quit their old job first," says Ted. "Joyce took the first step. She and her sister went on the road with the mobile bakery. We were separated for weeks at a time."

"I had to go to potentially dodgy places like carnivals," recalls Joyce of those early days. "The kids were worried even though they were pretty well grown. [Joyce is the doting stepmother to Ted's five children.] They were used to my being home."

Like the Fergusons, the Rices began to sell franchises. While they've never worked out that twenty-week work year, Ted and Joyce are far happier and wealthier than they were in their previous professional lives. "Sailing?" Joyce chuckles. "What's that? Maybe we'll get a chance to work part-time when we retire. Seriously, we're glad that T. J. Cinnamons is a success."

Many couples fantasize about running a romantic country inn, far away from the bustle of the city. Lin and Susan Simon are the proud owners of Wheatleigh, an elegant, private retreat set on the edge of the Tanglewood music center in Lenox, Massachusetts. Their roster of return guests reads like who's who in theatre and music. Among those who frequent Wheatleigh's antique-filled bedrooms and award-winning dining room are Billy Joel, Yo-Yo Ma, Paul Newman, Bill Murray, and Martha Graham. The Simons met in high school, and had varied careers in academia and antique dealing while they raised their children. Wheatleigh's tranquil gardens hardly bespeak the intensity of effort that the couple puts out to keep this famous hideaway in top form.

Susan smiles. "Lin and I don't have time for a mid-life crisis. There aren't enough hours in the day with the hotel and three teenage daughters."

"Running a small luxury property isn't something we jumped into," admits Lin. "We had been married for quite some time, having a number of different professions. I've always been the black sheep of my family. I have a Harvard law degree, which I used to study American history and buy a country hotel. Susan and I feel that Wheatleigh suits our personalities and attitudes."

None of these couples sat up in bed at night dreaming of total togetherness in the workplace. In fact, nearly all the couples we interviewed insisted that periods of soloing and separate work zones were what kept them and their enterprises going.

Karen and David Waltuck have won numerous accolades for their extraordinary cuisine. Their Lower Manhattan restaurant, Chanterelle, is one of a handful of consistent multi-starred survivors in a city of fickle palates. Recently, the pair had to pull up roots and relocate. It was their first true career trauma since the restaurant opened to instant raves in 1979. (In intensely competitive New York City, the expensive restaurant that remains hot for ten years is rare indeed.) Unlike most longtime co-preneurs, the Waltucks went into business together from the moment they said "I do."

"It seemed very natural for us to open the restaurant," says Karen while she nurses their first baby in Chanterelle's spare and elegant anteroom. "I was in retail and David was already a professional chef. He majored in marine biology at college, but his first love's always been cooking. While we were dating, his crazy chef's hours were fun, but when we decided to marry, we thought, why not do this for ourselves? That way, we could have more compatible schedules. I don't know how anyone could run a restaurant without having the spouse involved. You'll never see them, otherwise."

At the same time, Karen acknowledges that she and David are so divided in their labors that there's no problem with too much day-to-day proximity. "It's like having two jobs in the same company. I'm the business side—and he's the chef. At night, we all eat together in the dining room, and then I'm in the front of the house until closing. David gets reports on what's going on in the dining room, but that's my territory. Which is how we both want it. David's still quite shy about talking to people, and even at home, I can't even scramble an egg. We have about the same amount of private time together as most busy couples who work at separate places. In fact, we have to talk shop at home, because it's the only place that we're together without others around making demands on our time."

Joan and David Helpern, whose shoe and now handbag designs are featured in the finest department and specialty fashion stores, including over one hundred Ann Taylor branches, told us that without Joan's routine trips to their Italian factory, the couple would probably experience more tension at home. Says Joan about these regular breaks, "It saved our marriage. My trips give us breathing spells. When I come back, David and I feel a renewed sense of romance."

David admits, "I like the fact that she travels."

"Even though I always have jet lag," Joan groans.

While David was already involved in fashion and retail, his energetic wife had her own separate career path in education and child psychology. Before marrying David, she was director of child development for the New York City Board of Education. "I, too, had planned to be in education," says David. "But then came World War II. Afterwards, I decided to go into business."

After the death of his first wife, David met Joan through friends. They married after a six-week courtship. Today, they supervise twenty-two Italian factories and have recently expanded their line to include handbags, belts, and other leather accessories. Joan and David's credo is that fashion should reflect the customer's needs. They've built their business along the same low-key sensible line.

None of the aforementioned couples expected to develop thriving companies without some moments of personal touch-and-go. All admit that without a rock-steady relationship to start, the strain of the co-preneurial life might have pushed them over the edge. As Joan Helpern puts it, "When you choose to work with your spouse, you'd better make sure that your marriage is working."

But even partners who are endlessly devoted to each other's success should think carefully before hanging up a dual shingle.

Dr. Shirley Zussman thinks that latent competitive feelings are brought to the fore when married partners incorporate. "There are still many male/female ego tussles that need to be addressed," she warns.

One respected married pediatric care team ran into professional trouble when the wife, a Ph.D. and a therapist, became more popular with patients than her M.D. husband. "I wasn't the one who had to give out the bad news or stick the children with needles," she says. "I did the counseling and offered emotional comforting. The parents and kids naturally preferred my style to that of my husband."

Her spouse began to react by telling patients not to listen to his wife's advice because she lacked an M.D. This battle of egos carried over into their private lives to the point that the couple is currently separated.

"You would think that someone in my field would be able to get a handle on this sort of situation." The therapist sighs. "But when it comes to your own backyard . . ."

Even couples who appear to be getting along in their marriages should pose themselves the following questions before marketing those granola cookies or starting a desktop publishing newsletter.

- How well did each of you get along with your own family while growing up? Did you find it relatively easy to take part in chores and projects with parents and siblings? Were you more jealous than usual when a brother or sister achieved success?
- Do you and your spouse have a high efficiency level when it comes to handling your personal business affairs? Marriage, with its endless stream of joint domestic and financial responsibilities, is a paradigm of business management. If one of you is the primary organizer, how easily could you teach the other the ropes? Would the other partner be willing to learn?
- What skills and talents would each of you bring to the venture? Are your potential contributions complementary, or would there be a fair amount of overlapping?
- Seeing each other in a professional as well as personal

dimension has two sides. How would each of you feel if you saw the other acting in a professional context that made you bristle? Could you accept your spouse's management style even if it differed from your own?

- Could you and your partner engage in a three-hour negotiating session with a potential client on Friday and still be able to make love on Saturday morning? Husbands and wives can become desexed through too much work contact.

- Are there currently shared activities in your marriage that have nothing to do with your work lives? It's critical to have outside interests that allow both of you to spend time together away from the shop.

- What are your motivations for going into business? What does each of you expect to gain from working together? How similar are your goals for the future?

- If you have children, how will this change affect your family life? Do you see your offspring making a contribution? How do you think you'll react if older children show little or no interest in your company?

- Are you and your spouse able to evaluate situations and accept failure without blaming the other? Is each of you prepared professionally in case the venture does not succeed, or the other partner wants out? What might such a decision do to your feelings for your mate?

- Is each of you equally committed to the enterprise? Does your loyalty to each other supersede devotion to your company's success?

THE LOOK OF LOVE BEATS THE COLOR OF MONEY

Even if you haven't worked out the dynamics of the first nine co-preneuring questions, the tenth should be a shout-it-from-the rooftops *YES*.

The marriage of jewelry entrepreneurs Angela and Bruce Cummings was literally made in Tiffany's. He was a rising executive with the store; she, recently arrived from Germany, was a young designer destined for greatness. When the pair eventually married, Tiffany's was perfectly delighted. But the Cummingses were less enthusiastic about the legendary store's new management, and so they left to start up their own fine jewelry and design company. Their priorities have always been clear.

"Business is like a game. You're always going to make a few wrong moves," asserts Angela. "But marriage isn't a game. Decisions there are different."

Bruce believes that their work partnership flourishes because they've always been a couple first—long before they even thought about going into business. "Angela and I worked in completely different offices and areas of Tiffany's. The romance began from a mutual attraction, not proximity."

"He could have been a truck driver—I just *had* to meet him!" she adds with a knowing smile.

Henny and Berge Santo are part of the family team that owns and operates a group of New York's most famous and long-lived restaurants, including Sign of the Dove and Yellowfingers. Their more recent additions, Arizona 206 and Contrapunto, are always packed with the city's gourmets. The Santo family has even opened a bakery within blocks of their four establishments. Henny and Berge run the "flagship" Sign of the Dove, which has recently regained the kudos of serious culinary critics. Henny recently gave birth to the couple's third child.

"I thought the restaurant business was crazy," says Henny, laughing. "I've been in the business for five years. I do all the advertising and public relations as well as the day-to-day floor management of the Dove. I have a rather eclectic career background," she adds in what would appear to be an understatement. "I've ghosted syndicated columns for major publications, run a clinic for obese women, and I used to operate a private detective agency for lawyers."

Berge is pleased that his wife has officially joined the team. "I've taken on a different role since Henny's been here. I've become a sort of fireman." He admits that the pair do not always see eye to eye. "We have differences on policies and employees. No matter how 'right' Henny may be, there are times I have to dominate. Most of these problems stem from a difference in personality. Henny will want someone in and I won't, or vice versa. Who's going to make the decision? That's a decision unto itself."

"We were married a long time before we started working together. We're quite familiar with each other's foibles," says Henny. "But our relationship, although much of it is now tied up with the restaurant, is definitely anchored by our family life."

Couples like the Cummingses and the Santos hold their private moments in high regard. Says Henny of her husband and business partner, "He's an active father. Berge can take time off for the class trip—and he does. We have a good nanny, but both of us try and do as much as possible with the kids. We leave our apartment at different times, so the children see us both. We feel strongly about not wasting our free time together with people whom we'd really rather not see. I won't spend an evening off that makes me unhappy."

Adds Berge, "I don't want to hear too much about my business from acquaintances. Our true friends don't take advantage. They understand that we're running a restaurant company to make a living, not as a personal indulgence. If someone we know comes here for dinner, we might say hello or send over some wine, but, otherwise, we have to get to work."

TWO HEADS ARE BETTER THAN ONE DESK

Henny Santo: "We don't share offices or a secretary."

Angela Cummings: "Bruce is the one who comes into New York every day. I'm usually at my home studio in Connecticut."

Karen Waltuck: "If I see David for more than a few minutes during a busy night, that's a lot."

Giving each other enough breathing, creating, or computing room is one of the successful co-preneuring couple's best secrets. Even if you and your partner start out small, it's necessary to delineate certain spaces. Which doesn't mean that you can't swap work zones or won't occasionally find yourselves feeling slightly cramped. How much physical space you'll need depends upon your chosen business and tolerance for proximity.

If you're fulfilling a service from your home (e.g., a mail order or product search company), you'll probably want to rethink your guest room into a work center. If the receiving of goods is involved, start thinking about renting storage as well as office space. Many grass roots ventures, like T. J. Cinnamons and Diet Center, were born at home but moved out as soon as profits permitted.

Cara and Artie run a growing catalog-finding service. Their attractive home in a St. Louis suburb isn't, as one might expect, cluttered with paper and equipment. A lone laptop sits closed on an antique rolltop desk. There's a fax machine and a file cabinet—all of it together in a compact corner of their large living room.

Artie is vice president of sales for a major chain of menswear stores. "My boss knows that we've started this business. He's actually the one who's giving us office space in exchange for future equity."

The pair began their enterprise when Cara couldn't find a certain type of sweater she wanted in any of the well-known catalogs.

The couple polled a number of friends and co-workers. "Almost everyone had gone through a similar experience. Catalog shopping is so vast today—it's impossible to keep up without clogging your mailbox or tearing pages out of every magazine. What we do, for an annual fee, is search out catalogs that meet a client's needs," explains Artie.

Though they've only been in business for a single year, the couple has already moved most of their work into a nearby two-room setup at Artie's office. "We can access anything we need right here at home," says Cara.

Artie confesses that seeing a mountain of catalogs and

printouts spilling onto the bedroom floor interfered with more than housekeeping. "We had decided to keep the living and dining areas free from clutter so we could entertain." He grins. "But whenever we started to make love, the first thing I would think about was taking care of clients."

Sexual intimacy isn't the only consideration in establishing a work space away from home. Small children, while wonderful morale boosters, can be disruptive. So can delivery people, neighbors, and even spouses!

If your enterprise, such as providing public relations counsel, publishing a newsletter, baking fruitcakes, or teaching piano or weaving, does feel more "at home" in your own domain, make certain that each of you has enough privacy to conduct your part of the business. Shared responsibility shouldn't preclude a room (or corner) of one's own.

DIVIDE AND CONQUER

In a 1989 *Wall Street Journal* article about co-preneurs and their struggles, reporter Barbara Marsh interviewed couples whose productivity took a backseat to bitter arguments about who was going to do what . . . and when . . . and how well. These partners hadn't anticipated the need to very specifically divvy up responsibilities. Power struggles emerged, along with divergent management styles and levels of energy and enthusiasm for the task at hand.

"Couples who work together need more than enough physical space—they should have separate responsibilities, too," advises Dr. Zussman. "Each partner should have distinct duties. The division of labor relieves stress and enhances each person's sense of achievement. This is why having enough diversity in your joint talent pool is so important."

Although Donna Karan and her husband don't really consider themselves co-preneurs, she has strong feelings about bringing a diversity of professional assets to such a relationship.

"Complementary skills? Absolutely! I wouldn't be in

business without Stephan. He understands things about me that I don't even understand myself. He thinks in terms of long-range planning—I tend to focus on now. He sees our company from the business point of view while I look at the more creative aspects. It's a real relief to know that someone is watching my company from my point of view. This really frees me to design," stresses Karan.

Adds husband Stephan Weiss, "Donna's helped me learn to go for it—to take chances and envision a dream. I think that from me, she's learned how to be more organized and disciplined."

"He's helped me to mature as an executive," Karan explains.

Ted Rice remembers the early days. "It was a major revelation. Everything focused on getting the job done. Each of us excelled at different things. The hard decision was whether to moonlight or go all the way. An entrepreneur is usually someone who has done many unrelated jobs. They can draw on everything they've learned."

"Couples need to understand that each is an individual with his or her own skills and approaches. The other spouse must learn to respect that," says Joyce. "It's also healthy to have separate hobbies and interests away from work. Ted has his ham radio—I have my music."

Co-preneurs who ease rather than leap into their roles find that carving out territories of responsibility comes easily. Ed Safdie, founder of the famed Green House, the Sonoma Mission Inn, and owner of the Norwich Inn & Spa in Connecticut, worked in real estate development and sales long before Carlene, his wife of twenty-four years, joined the company on an active basis.

"We divide up our work almost all the time," says Ed. "Carlene is involved in the aesthetic decisions at Norwich. Her taste is great—I hardly even check in with what's going on unless she calls me. She doesn't need my okay to order curtain fabric or consult with the chef. When I was involved with investment banking, she was part of the emotional team. This is the logical extension of that."

Carlene Safdie also oversees design and production of the lavish cookbooks that are based on the Safdies' elegant but sensible approach to healthy dining. "I do the deal—she does the rest," says Ed.

"You have to think of each other as associates and not take each other for granted," he emphasizes. "Many couples are too used to each other's responses. It takes work to readjust your reactions."

Joan Helpern talks about how she came over to her husband's field. "We were challenged about going into shoes. I paint, so design came easily to me. New England is the center of the footwear industry. I saw what manufacturers were proposing for women and I laughed. I knew, even in 1964, that women would be working as executives and want something different. Why shouldn't we do it ourselves? I was getting my Ph.D. at Harvard. I designed shoes at night. When David went to work in the morning, I yelled, 'Wait for me!' "

The pair's business went through several changes of name and distribution before the Coty Award-winning Joan & David became established. Throughout those years, both of them found their respective business niches.

"Building a working relationship is critical," says Joan as she pats Bijou, their enormous, ever-present bichon frise. "David could take over my functions and vice versa, but it would be dumb."

As Dr. Zussman points out, creating individual areas where each person has the potential to excel can relieve some of the stress caused by feelings of competition. Other psychological scenarios can also come into positive or negative focus, depending upon the rest of the marital relationship. "There's the problem of the student/teacher roles and who plays them," she says.

Jeff Clyman was delighted when his wife felt secure enough to venture onto his corporate turf. "It was great that Jacky negotiated a deal that I normally would have done. Not only did I take pride in her success and my ability to 'teach' what I had learned myself from experience, but it was a relief. If anything ever happened to me, Jacky could carry on."

Roger and Sybil Ferguson had to sort out where each of their best talents lay. Says Roger, "A strong ego can be a problem. Sybil would tell me that we had to take certain steps for the clients' sake. I would evaluate the cost. Sometimes I would say no, and she would disagree. It took me a while to accept her judgment in some cases, and for her to see my financial point of view."

Berge and Henny Santo are another couple whose strong wills have been willingly tempered by a mutual need to learn from each other. "Berge is so much calmer about life," says Henny. "He's taught me to be tougher and more rational. I can fight my own battles."

Henny has used her successful role as the restaurant's public voice to convince her husband to show his face a bit more. "She's made me a better communicator," admits Berge. "I was asked to do a TV interview. Without Henny's persuading, I wouldn't have seen the importance of doing it."

ALL IN THE FAMILY?

One of the more important questions on the co-preneurs' preparedness list is how they feel about bringing offspring into the business. While this generation of parents may be emotionally equipped to face their children's self-determination, parents who create their own empires, large or small, still have those hand-me-down fantasies.

Dr. Zussman cautions about taking too strong a position either way. "On the one hand, children can show no interest. Yet a family company can provide a place where children learn to build their lives. It's critical that you see them as people unto themselves—don't fall into the wish-fulfillment trap of waiting for the day when they'll take over."

The Fergusons never suffered from chronic professional infighting until their adult son expressed an interest in taking over as acting president. Roger looks back on that awkward time. "We always felt that family came first. When our son ran the store, it became uncomfortable. He wanted to do certain things in a way which Sybil and I felt were not good for Diet Center. We couldn't change his mind and we couldn't fire him. There was a loss of discipline. Ultimately, he stepped down and struck out on his own venture. He wanted the experience of being an entrepreneur so that he'd know what to do with his own product. All of us learned the hard way."

Family business experts claim that fewer than one-third of family-owned companies make it into the second generation. And only about half of that group succeeds to be managed by a third generation.

While the Santo children are still too young for any kind of an active role in their business, Berge clearly gets a kick from their interest. "Our nine-year-old does restaurant reviews and actually set up a mock restaurant at his school. The four-year-old came up with the solution to a problem I was having."

Henny nods. "We think the kids should have a say, but they're so young yet. Certainly we're not going to force any of them to take over. Right now, the benefit is that they understand why we have irregular hours. They appreciate what we do."

Ted Rice stresses firmly, "Don't set up a business for your kids. What if they don't want to do the work, or can't handle the job?"

Joyce agrees. "When my daughter worked directly for me, there was a good deal of tension, though it generally worked out. We told all the children that they didn't have to stay with the business unless they really wanted to."

Adds Ted, "Don't sacrifice yourself for your spouse or your kids. Be honest about your enthusiasm. If family members want to get involved, draw them a realistic picture."

KEEPING PERSONAL PACE WITH YOUR PROFESSIONAL SELVES

All of the partners in this chapter are doing extremely well with their chosen enterprises . . . and their marriages.

That's because, whether or not they're aware of it, each set of spouses plays by the rules of Power Partnership.

In order for their businesses and relationships to grow apace, co-preneurs must be flexible and philosophical about their special situation. Designers Angela and Bruce Cummings know that diamonds aren't a successful couple's best friend.

Bruce sums up what he thinks is the bedrock of the co-preneuring lifestyle. "You really have to be committed to building a business and a marriage because there are so many ups and downs. It's not 'Oh, that looks like fun, let's try it!' Too many successful couples start believing their own press. They think they're so neat."

Says Angela, "These people don't put enough into the marriage itself. I've been giving talks on that subject. This isn't something light. Bruce and I built a business, a house, and had a baby at the same time. That takes doing."

Knowing *who* you are and *what* you want keeps the two of you from feeling overwhelmed by sudden growth or a change of gears.

Sybil Ferguson concurs. "We've always had to keep up with Diet Center. We were actually worried about growing too fast and going broke. We had a tiger by the tail. Our Mormon faith and love for each other helped. Roger and I really went into this so that people could lose weight and feel better about themselves. That's still very important to us, as is quality of life. We have a child care center at our main office; we think of our franchisees and employees as extended family members. We go off to the mountains and get spiritually in touch with ourselves. You've got to make your own support system and keep that healthy, too."

Karen Waltuck thinks it important that a couple have mutual goals. "When you succeed, one partner may feel that he or she can leave the marriage and go off on their own. I don't think that a strong relationship is ruined by having a good business, as long as you both want the same end results. I would always want to work with my husband, even if he decided to try something different. Right now, we enjoy our work. We're not out to prove anything. If David wanted to use Chanterelle as a jumping-off point to selling a line of products, we might have some trouble. But neither of us feels that way."

Says David, "We're the same people after getting four stars."

Ed Safdie feels that couples who work together should try and be honest with themselves about the negatives; he even suggests that they can be turned around. "Everybody has tensions—who's kidding themselves? Carlene and I aren't just together at dinner. We're in contact all day. If you take the right approach, all of that communication can ease the stress. Keeping in touch can dissipate the smaller problems."

Ted Rice echoes his sentiments. "I think people should spend less time coping and more time doing. Don't worry so much—forget that stuff and figure out solutions. Then you can look forward to solving the difficulties."

A NOT-SO-PRIVATE ENTERPRISE

One recent book has referred to co-preneuring as "The Glorious Dream," painting a rosy picture of life that completely disregards the truths our own couples have embraced. (For example, the idea that both partners must be equally passionate about the venture is put down as a "myth.") Instead, readers of this volume were encouraged simply to rely on "love decisions." (Interestingly, not a single couple whose experience was cited was willing to be identified.) According to this view, love, and love alone, will find a way.

"Tell me about it," snaps Jacky Clyman. "I was having dinner with our seven-year-old and an adult friend. I asked my son if it bothered him that I worked along with Daddy. He replied, 'Work keeps your mind occupied. It's good for you, Mommy.' At first I was flabbergasted, but he actually meant just what he said. It made me realize how ready you have to be for all kinds of responses."

Jeff laughs. "When we were getting married, I wasn't sure about that—right up until the night before. Marriage is an evolutionary experience, and so is work. Everything continues—there's no simple start or stop. When two people have a real business, others become involved. We try and treat our employees the way we would ourselves. You can't love or work in a vacuum."

Adds Jacky, "However close two people are in marriage or business, they cannot assume the responsibility of being each other's *only* best friend. There must be some buffers."

Angela and Bruce Cummings feel similarly, and have hired a manager who gives each of them criticism and advice. Henny and Berge Santo must consult with Berge's older brother, Joseph. Lin and Susan Simon are already thinking about who will manage Wheatleigh in the years ahead. Joan and David Helpern rely on their carefully chosen executive team to keep up the company's high standards of production and distribution.

To paraphrase the angel Clarence in *It's a Wonderful Life*, one co-preneur's life touches so many others. Those "others" include your children, parents, friends, employees, accountants, suppliers, and the one that you lead together during those rare moments when you leave your professional selves behind. Be prepared for the unusual and unexpected. As Joan Helpern wisely asserts, "Normal life is not like a book."

Those "love decisions" won't be of much use when the inventory is two weeks late or the FDA decrees that you must change the formula of your herbal dandruff treatment. What will pull you through are *commonsense decisions* based on your respect for each other and for what you're both trying to accomplish. As with raising children, never anticipate perfection or be afraid to seek outside help. Your marriage and business are too important to leave in the hands of an amorphous fate. There's nothing romantic about calling lawyers, whether for bankruptcy or divorce.

WHAT THEY DID FOR LOVE AND . . .

All Power Partners can learn from successful co-preneurs. These are men and women whose love and trust in each other's instincts are so strong that they're willing to bet their precious careers on them. Many people enjoy working for such couples because their loyalty and integrity levels often rise above that of the average vice president, or even CEO, who was essentially elected to power.

What do these couples get from undertaking such personal risks and responsibilities? Many of them, though less than thoroughly satisfied at their jobs, were doing well, and could easily have looked for better and more challenging positions in their fields.

Talk with couples like Karen and David Waltuck or Joan and David Helpern, and the answer becomes a bit clearer. These pairs knew that the intensity of their individual work commitments might give them a chance to use their co-mentoring abilities in the most personal way possible.

Co-preneuring *isn't* for everyone; some of the most committed Power Partners can't take the heat in the same kitchen. Those who are most comfortable being supportive and loving when the other mate's problems don't mirror their own should definitely not apply. Nor should couples who are still learning how to delegate responsibility in their own homes. Co-preneuring is a terrific way to discover new skills and strengths—it's a terrible and costly method of teaching marital teamwork.

If the two of you know what it is that you want from your marriage and careers, and have put in adequate time on both with good results thus far . . . co-preneuring could work out in your mutual favor.

Dr. Shirley Zussman fondly recalls the period of her professional and personal life when she and her now-deceased husband, Leon, a leading New York gynecologist, shared a practice in sexual therapy.

"It was very exciting. My husband and I got so much out of working as a team. I loved it, even though there were some problems. In the beginning, I thought that I was the 'great therapist,' but there were many times that Leon's interpretations were more on target than my own!"

She continues, "We shared victories and defeats together. This was good for our patients. Sometimes, they would actually get to see us working out our own viewpoints. Occasionally, something personal would slip out and we would disagree during a therapy session. Patients, especially those who had trouble communicating with each other, would see us negotiate ourselves out of the dispute. I really think that co-preneuring skills are important to learn now because cottage industries will be the wave of the future. Many of these couples will be working at home."

As we've been saying all along, shared victories are usually the best. Partners whose victories stem from a shared professional endeavor have the opportunity to add a special dimension to their personal lives.

"A co-preneur couple should strive for consensus," says Bruce Cummings.

His wife, Angela, adds, "Selfishness is the worst trait to have in a marriage or business. You must learn to give up some things that you want at the moment in order to gain what you want later on."

Susan Simon offers this advice: "Be honest about what you can and can't do. Or what you want to do. Accept the fact that there'll be times when you can't share everything. I'm jealous of Lin's money sense, and there are times he can't understand exactly what I'm doing with art or furnishings. But this doesn't stop us looking forward to more success."

And Ed Safdie addresses living with the differences and harnessing their advantages: "I don't believe that married work partners speak the same language. That's how they keep their independence. One partner may be the hard edge, the other is the soft voice. Yet each one knows when to let the other step forward. That's what makes co-preneuring so satisfying."

Nice work if you can get it!

7

THE PLEASURES (AND PERILS) OF POINTS

•

Throughout this book, we've been showing you how to develop marital strengths that will lead you toward your chosen personal goals. But *attaining* success is only the first set in the whole match. Living with success requires a special kind of Power Partnering. Trump cards can actually destroy the day-to-day pleasure of playing the game, especially if you haven't mapped out a joint success strategy in advance. Winning becomes a frightening prospect for the unprepared.

Advancement means change. The fishbowl gets bigger. Travel and longer periods of separation may become part of the bargain. Each spouse may be tempted to make more demands on the other. Some dependable acquaintances will try to use their access to you for personal gain.

While you and your spouse are ascending together, the thrill of moving progressively skyward is exhilarating. But what if one partner starts to accelerate beyond the couple's comfort threshold?

These consequences must be faced as directly as those

associated with failure. Few couples ever think that getting hold of the gold ring could bode anything but good fortune for their relationship. But consider how few leaders of industry or entertainment superstars are *still married* to their initial spouses.

As discussed earlier, keeping up the pace is part of the challenge. But it's the more complex issue of losing empathy and affection that severs nuptial vows with an unexpected vengeance; career advancement can be the unkindest cut of all. The successful couples in this book have had to face their "moments of marital truth" in the face of rapid professional growth.

Some of them realized that common burnout from too much traveling on the part of one or both partners was the primary threat. Others found themselves in the unwanted position of competing *with* instead of *for* each other. A few had to grapple with hidden pockets of reverse gender jitters. Those whose words appear here opted for the marriage first, even if it meant sorting out heated emotions that had previously been packed in cold storage.

Part of loving someone is accepting defeats and shortcomings. Many people are better suited to hand-holding when the chips are down than they are to applauding when it comes to cashing in.

Our culture encourages constant achievement. The underside is that even when we succeed, there is always *more pressure* not to rest on our laurels—even for a single day of celebration.

Success also promotes an insidious syndrome whereby the thrill of achievement becomes stronger than the marriage bond. These couples become addicted to their own and each other's accomplishments. Instead of using a period of expansion to create a more dynamic intimacy, they throw away everything else in their lives for the sake of staying at the top. These pressures usually take their toll in the bedroom sooner rather than later.

Partners in tune with each other's goals don't work for points in a vacuum. They consider the ramifications of each single or double opportunity lost—and won. Communication can provide a sensible perspective from the peaks as well as the valleys. As you will see, so does every other partnering skill that you've been mastering on the tough road to the top.

ISOLATION AND ENVY: ALL ALONE TOGETHER

It isn't always easy for a spouse to accept a partner's unanticipated professional elevation. While the outward trappings of rapid achievement can look attractive, once the reality of increased social and professional responsibility sinks in, new pressures emerge. Some of them pose serious problems that can whittle away at otherwise strong unions. Leon Botstein admits that his appointment, at age twenty-eight, to Bard College's presidency contributed to the breakup of his first marriage.

"My wife couldn't face the change in relationships with those around us," he explains. "We were young, yet we couldn't go off with graduate students, faculty members, and everyone else in our own age group. I was the president of the college and she was my spouse. People started to treat us deferentially, and we were expected to behave differently with our peers. She felt isolated and angry. She couldn't offer sympathy or encouragement when I felt disheartened because of the way she perceived my success.

"Barbara was an early achiever like myself. She understands how even those near or at the top of their professions can feel inadequate and discouraged. Our relationship has been strengthened by our early successes and the isolation from our contemporaries that it sometimes caused."

Jerry Della Femina also admits that his sudden spurt of professional gain played a part in ending his initial union.

"We were very young kids from Brooklyn. Moving to Manhattan was a big deal. The trouble was that I had to start going out with clients. I wanted a strong spouse at my side—I wanted a real partner. My wife wouldn't come along or grow with me. It's extremely difficult to do what I do without someone else there to share the load . . . and the fun."

Though more professionally determined men encourage their partners to keep up the pace, some continue to find a cloud-climbing female companion overwhelming.

Nick Ashford remembers his jealousy when Valerie Simpson was asked to record a solo album. "Even though we weren't yet married, we had become extremely close, both emotionally and professionally. For the first time, I began to experience bad feelings about her possibly pulling ahead of me. It almost broke up the partnership."

Valerie remembers those times, too. "Maybe I wasn't aware enough of Nick's feelings. I was younger, and got carried away with all of the sudden attention. As it turned out, my great solo career was a dud—that helped bring us back together." Neither Nick nor Valerie knows what would happen should such an opportunity arise for either of them today.

As Nick explains, "Our music is what binds us together spiritually. We commune through our art. In my mind, that was threatened by her working completely without me. I just don't know if I would have the same intense reaction. We haven't had to deal with that as yet."

Some spouses fear that success will ruin their loved one's personality or change their values. Instead of offering support and attempting a growth spurt of his or her own, the terrified partner contemplates ways to curb the size of the other's forward leap. He or she begins to set up unwarranted roadblocks. "We can't move to Los Angeles because I can't drive." Or "It's too bad that this had to come up now—right in the middle of the kids' school year."

Never mind that the new job package includes a chauffeured car and that at age forty-two, it's about time you got your license. As for the disrupted school year, no one ever said that the company wouldn't allow your spouse to commute for six months, or that by next year, the older child will be in college.

Other fearful husbands and wives attempt to create self-doubt in the mind of the successful spouse. They belittle their partner's ability to cope with the advancement. Instead of reacting to good news with anticipation and exhilaration, these spouses send out warning signals of impending personal doom. "I'll bet you won't last six months as publisher—you know how poorly you manage people." "Great—and what am I supposed to do while you're running off to Paris and Milan for weeks at a time? We don't need any more money—why can't you just say that you're happier doing the domestic buying? You can't even speak French!"

Entrepreneur and former Mobil Corporation executive Judith Moncrieff is married to Gamble Baldwin, a successful businessman twenty years her senior. His professional self-assurance played a major role in their getting together.

"Many men in my own age group thought I was too threatening. I didn't see myself married because I needed someone who saw me as an equal. I wanted to marry my best friend . . . and I did. Gamble and I can accept each other's independence. In many ways he's 'younger' than I am; he's the person who's taught me how to let go."

"I've always wanted Judith to have an important enough job," replies Gamble. "I'm not the type to attach strings to a relationship."

The pair has always been supportive of any career change that can bring new challenges. "Gamble had a good offer from First Boston at a time when he was doing well at a much smaller firm. I told him to go for it—even though it could have meant risking our relationship. Now, Gamble is letting me take a chance with my new company. He was thrilled when my patent for FlexAddress came through."

Dr. Zussman asserts that couples have to look at these forward moves from both sides. "Recognize success as a two-part deal. The person who gets promoted often fails to understand why his or her mate isn't as enthusiastic. It never occurs to them that the other's dreams may not be exactly the same."

There are times, Dr. Zussman believes, that "you shouldn't accept the golden opportunity. The person concerned has an obligation to weigh it against the needs of the entire family. If a change in lifestyle, especially a physical move, is going to be too upsetting, the increase in salary or status may not be worth the potential stress."

SEX, LIES, AND CEOS

A sudden surge of success can make you feel sixteen again—ready to conquer the universe before lunch. But think about other adolescent responses. Cautions Dr. Zussman, "When the teacher gives you an A after you've been getting C+'s, you begin worrying that if Mr. or Miss Murphy knew what you had been really thinking about during the test, you wouldn't be rewarded for your efforts.

"The person who is catapulted has doubts about deserving the honor. That individual needs to examine from where these feelings arise and how to prevent them from getting in the way of future achievements. Here is where a supportive spouse can be especially helpful. And if that partner is acutely aware of what it took to reach the goal, so much the better for both of them. Neither will make disproportionate sexual or emotional demands on the other."

Dr. Zussman recalls the problems faced by a youthful CEO and his wife. "Everyone fussed over him at functions and in his company because he was strong and personable. He was perceived as being great at everything. Only in the bedroom did his spouse seize control. She became so demanding during sex that he actually became afraid of her. He never allowed himself to reveal vulnerability at any other time. His mate felt overwhelmed by the supposed aura of power around him. She needed to still feel in charge of some part of their life together."

She adds, "Sometimes success deprives one or both partners of adequate personal attention. Men and women are equally needy in this area. No one wants to play second emotional fiddle to a spouse's job, no matter how many benefits may come with it."

Not all couples are comfortable with lavish lifestyles,

either. Dr. Zussman recalls an instance where the man literally made his fortune overnight. "He was small in stature and kept buying bigger and bigger houses and boats. Most of us would kill for an indoor swimming pool—his wife would say to me, 'Having all this stuff is a barrier to having good friends.' She was actually the partner who was less insecure about the sudden wealth. It was the man who felt the need to show off. We all know what Freud might have said about that," she reminds us.

"In contrast, I recently attended a hospital fund-raiser where most of the women were elegantly dressed. The wealthiest woman in the room, a hardworking professional, was the only one not wearing massive diamonds and a drop-dead outfit. This was a person who, perhaps because of her job, had come to accept her husband's position as nothing more than a part of everyday life. Status meant nothing except being able to donate more money and have more input into causes which they both cared about."

Another variation on this problem is the spouse who cares more about "keeping up" than the partner who got them there in the first place. Kevin, a boyish investment banker, longs to cash out for a few years and start an inner-city business school in downtown Miami. "But my wife just wants to keep going and going . . . all the way to the snootiest enclave in Palm Beach. She thinks that we can buy our way into the *Social Register*. Who cares? We were never poor, but somehow life seemed easier when we both had to work to afford the extras. I always thought that if I struck it rich, her not working would mean taking off time to have kids. That I would understand."

As wealth and social influence increase, a difference in a couple's individual values can emerge. Each spouse begins to see success in a different light. One partner may want to move into a completely new world of people and experiences; the other might prefer to remain in the current environment and hold court as a "big fish" in a middle-class pond. Each may also secretly harbor anxieties about added fiscal responsibilities that come with such upward swings of fortune.

RUNNING MATES

"People who strive for goals tend to be competitive. When you're exposed to someone whose aspirations are close to yours, tension will build. One partner may feel that he or she isn't putting in enough time or effort," says Dr. Zussman. "Competitive feelings spill over into the bedroom. The gung-ho executive can have deep insecurities about performance. If the female spouse has more career clout, the man may feel intimidated. Some men enjoy having wives who are perceived as professional tigers by the outside world; these same women are expected to be far more yielding during intimate moments.

"I can usually tell when a couple is having this problem of intramarital competition. During the early office sessions, they're sarcastic and angry. They bait each other constantly, trying to prove their individual superiority. What comes through is their joint frustration at not having enough time with each other."

Zussman tells such couples that they have to reestablish priorities. "What's the point of reaching the top of your profession when you end up sacrificing the pleasures of a loving relationship?"

Competition can bring a couple closer if their first priority is their personal relationship. Egging each other on can be part of productive teamwork, as long as the results benefit both partners. For instance, it's a fair assumption that couples whose finances are pretty much in one pot won't be as prone to jealousy if one of them gets a substantial salary increase or bonus.

·Judith Moncrieff thinks that many couples become competitive by not making time to advise each other. "You end up fighting over where and how time together is spent. It's hard work depressurizing a busy partner—especially when you're tired, too. You must work listening to each other's troubles into your schedule. Gamble and I have also learned that de-escalating a crisis sometimes means backing off."

Moncrieff and Baldwin have learned to give each other space where sharing the spoils is concerned. "Gamble likes to use some of our hard-earned 'mad money' to finance fishing trips here and abroad. While I know he would love to have me along, I also know that he is sensitive to the fact that I'm *not* the happy camper type. So he goes with a bunch of friends. I am spending some of our joint 'success' on launching my new business. You have to take time out and tell your partner that you appreciate his or her efforts and don't begrudge them their just desserts."

She adds knowingly, "And be sure to tell your partner how much he or she contributed to your win! Men want to feel a part of their wives' achievements as much as women want their loyalty and support. When you're running neck and neck, you shouldn't keep looking over your shoulder to see if you're being outpaced by your spouse—it should feel more like a relay race where each of you takes up the baton for part of the run. Sprints don't bring people together."

Occasionally, couples with similar or identical careers find themselves competing in public. Frank and Melinda Harmon were a married pair of Houston trial lawyers. (She's now a federal judge.) They had made a mutual pact never to appear against each other in the courtroom. Melinda admits that while lawyers, their competitive danger zone tended to be their own backyard.

"We solved that problem by never, ever talking about our work at home," she emphasizes. "Sometimes Frank was in trial and I was not even aware of it! I know that sounds odd, but it prevented all forms of competition and resentment."

Some partners engage in overwork competitions to avoid facing other precarious facets of their relationship. If you're too tired from a long day to make love, it's easier to avoid discussions about sexual techniques or whether to discard the diaphragm. Coming home extra late or leaving the house at dawn automatically dumps responsibilities like cleaning, household shopping, and getting children off to school in the other person's overburdened lap. It's surprisingly easy to fall into such a trap.

"I used to work at this weird public relations firm which employed mostly women. The joke around the office was that everyone stayed late to flirt with the unattached male boss," remembers Helen, who has since gone on to open her own successful consulting service. "I fell into this routine, even though I had a lot to come home to. My husband, who, as an actuary, keeps pretty tough hours himself, found this amusing. He even tried to make a game out of it—who's home first? The last one in the door was deemed the winner because he or she didn't have to cook. Naturally, we didn't have kids when we did this."

But the pair soon discovered that this kind of behavior began having a negative influence on other aspects of the marriage. Whoever came to bed last had to capitulate to the other's sexual requests. Whoever got up earlier on Saturday morning would have to do the week's primary food shopping. Instead of reacting as a team, Helen and her husband, Darryl, kept building up individual demands on each other.

"We literally kept challenging ourselves into separation," says Darryl. "It was kind of fun at first. But we took this ridiculous thing too far and ended up wasting a lot of time that we could have been spending together. I also started having negative fantasies about Helen and the rest of this 'harem' waiting their turn to be whisked into the backseat of the owner's stretch limo. Not that I didn't trust her, but . . ."

They finally confronted each other about the situation over lukewarm take-out Chinese food. "One of the activities we used to look forward to was coming home and making dinner together. Instead, here was my husband challenging me to an eating race to see who would have to clean up. That brought us to our senses."

The episode taught them an important lesson in the nick of time. "Darryl and I are far more aware of our hidden competitiveness. We now try to avoid situations where one or both of us will be tempted to shirk mutual responsibilities or avoid discussing subjects that might put one of us on edge. If there's a disagreement, we now bargain the situation out together instead of hiding behind a contest of wills."

Competitions, even those that have innocent beginnings, can quickly add stress and mistrust where it's needed least. There are some partners who swear that a competitive atmosphere at home adds to their marriage. These are couples who usually don't feel comfortable being each other's only company. In contrast, co-mentors are usually greedy for any time alone they can get for themselves—and they'd rather not waste it with empty domestic dueling. Outscoring your mate isn't the way to increase your own success rate—assimilate each other's strategies and you won't have to sacrifice your intimacy on the altar of victory.

These are among the more emotional issues couples confront when faced with moving ahead. But increasing tension can build from outside sources, too. Success has many mothers—and nearly as many manipulators thinking up ways to make the most of *your* hard-earned position. And then there is the increased responsibility itself. The more each of you shoulders, the greater the likelihood of separation periods. Power Partners, because of their constantly expanding personal communications skills, have found preferable, if not always perfect, routes around these two common problems.

BARTERING AND BULLYING

There's a terribly proper and elegant historian who's married to an advertising mover and shaker. She is as refined and subtle as her priceless Louise Nevelson mantelpiece—unless she wants coverage for her latest book or cultural project. When we asked her to share her marital experiences, she coyly demurred—but not before pleading for access to one of our spouses, a New York newspaper executive. A short time later, when asked a similar question by a major advertising weekly, she eagerly complied.

A California radio reporter remembers how she agreed to placate the pushy spouse of one of her husband's marketing clients. "Out of deference, I bit my tongue and told this not-so-charming woman that I would do a small spot on her sportswear line. A few weeks later, when I had finally gotten around to producing the segment, my mother died unexpectedly. To be polite, I called the designer to explain why it would take longer to get the story done. I had barely gotten the words out of my mouth when she snarled, 'So, I guess you won't be using me on the air!' Not a word of condolence or understanding. My husband was furious that I had even *felt* obligated to help her."

Bartering access to a mate can be tricky at best. This is not the same as the private networking we talked about earlier. Bartering access comes with strings—some of them perilously long and tangled.

You can't exactly call it blackmail, since the demanding party doesn't threaten . . . directly. But we all know that the menace to pull out of a partner's deal or withdraw funding from a venture is lurking within the access request.

Diane Levbarg-Klein has developed her own cool reply when someone comes on too strong about meeting her lawyer husband. "I remind them that they are speaking to Diane Levbarg—*not* Mrs. Martin Klein. Of course, if *I* suggest calling my husband about a request, that's different. The trick is to use the right tone of voice—very few people have ever tried that tactic on me twice." She laughs.

The best and safest course is to suggest getting in touch with the other partner directly; put the connection ball in their court. Tell your spouse about the overture and decide then and there how to handle it as a couple.

Gail Blanke and Jim Cusick have also run into this problem. "When this happens to one of us, the other usually acts interested in the pitch or request and then says politely, 'I'll certainly tell him (or her) about your idea.' And I do tell Jim, and he tells me. I'm usually open to calling the person back. If I can't help, I say so myself. To me, that's the only proper way to handle these types of situations."

She adds, "If Jim wants me to see or help someone who will be beneficial to him, I go along unless it really goes against the grain. My own personality makes it possible for me to respond this way quite naturally—I'm not afraid of pushing Jim a little if I really need the favor, either. But neither of us ever forces the other into a truly odious compromise. That's just not fair."

Barbara Walters is another famous media figure who, along with her influential husband, has to make peace with this dilemma.

"I don't consider it a problem if it's straightforward," she says. "It happens. People who know Merv ask him if I would speak here or there. He leaves that decision to me. Sometimes I am approached about potential business for him."

It may well be that the request is worth weighing. Not all access exchanges are sinister. But beware the ones where showing the way could lead you both down a treacherous garden path of obligation. Sometimes the thorns of commitment aren't worth accepting the bouquet—especially on each other's behalf, no matter how intoxicating it smells at a distance.

SUITCASE SPOUSES

For most two-career couples, becoming successful means hitting the road. In theory, the idea of living in towering hotels with complimentary breakfasts and indoor pools sounds great.

The depressing reality is that most of this "glamorous" travel consists of one- and two-nighters of round-the-clock meetings and contract signings. After the third or fourth outing, most executives, no matter how pleasant the surroundings, wish they could quite literally pack it in.

Even travels to exciting destinations like Tokyo and Paris aren't much more stimulating if they're over in seventy-two hours . . . and there's no one to share the new experiences or your $100-a-head gourmet dinner. There are also stresses for those you've left behind.

"It's really our only area of marital friction," admits health care economist Deborah Freund. "The trouble is that I travel too much and Tom doesn't travel nearly as often, unless we plan it way in advance."

For the past two summers, the couple have managed to combine long-term work and vacation ventures to Australia and the Far East. "I stayed on for two extra weeks this year." Tom chuckles. "I really did have some extra work and friends to see, but it was also valuable for Deb to see what it was like coping with an empty home and no support system upon arrival."

"Actually, the real issue is all of those two- and three-day hops to Detroit and Philadelphia which I have to make on a regular basis," says Deborah. "It really screws up a lot of our social plans, not to mention getting our new house fixed up. I've been meaning to go out with Tom and shop for wallpaper, but I'm too tired or preoccupied with tomorrow's lecture—or next week's trip."

While neither Tom nor Deborah feels that this strain will cause a deep or permanent rift in their relationship, each realizes that some changes will eventually have to be made. "This much travel is necessary for this stage in my career," says Deborah, "but I'm already thinking of how I can change the focus of what I do enough so that I'm not always on the road. Tom knows that these aren't pleasure trips. He's not jealous because he knows what a grind business travel is most of the time."

Eric and Monica, the suburban lawyers from chapter 1, suffer from a different kind of travel stress. "Eric's company always sends him far away on short notice," Monica complains. "These aren't short overnights or midweek stopovers to D.C. or even California. At three days' notice, he could be in Frankfurt or Hong Kong. We just never know when he's got to go."

The couple has a three-year-old child and steady live-in

help. But even this companionship doesn't keep Monica from becoming frustrated . . . and worried.

"You see all those terrorist bombings and mechanical failures on TV and pray. Eric often flies the same route as that Pan Am plane that blew up—in fact, he was scheduled to go that week, but there was a last-minute change. I know that I'm overreacting—I mean, you can get hit by a car just as easily, but your chances must go up if you travel that often."

None of that has stopped Monica and Eric from enjoying the fruits of his frequent-flier mileage. The up side has been several first-class trips to Europe that the pair can make themselves at the last minute because of their excellent household help and flight status on major carriers.

"I'll admit that it was nice to be able to hop over to Ireland for a friend's wedding. The whole four-day weekend cost us less than $500. And even some of that was spent on Waterford crystal and smoked salmon." Monica smiles. "But I'd rather fly economy if it meant having Eric home at least eight consecutive weekends."

Eric admits that he is close to landing a plum position at another major company whose travel demands will keep him a great deal closer to home, even when he's on the move.

Road warriors also suffer from stress. If you're Paul and Linda McCartney, you have the resources to hire a private jet to take you home for short breaks between gigs. If you're the CEO of a major company (or one of his or her chosen VPs), there may be a helicopter at your disposal. There are also special private "homelike" facilities and corporate clubs available to upper management. These and other travel detraumatizers can't completely eradicate jet lag or isolation anxieties, but they help.

If you're not as yet a member of the traveling elite, there are still ways to improve the situation. Leading quality hotel companies that court both business and family travelers, such as Radisson Hotels International, have developed reduced-rate room plans to encourage professionals on the move to stay over a weekend and send for their spouse and children. Rates are competitively low, so the incentive is high.

Harriet Craig Peterson, vice president of marketing for Radisson Hotels International, sees both sides of the issue—as a hotel executive and as a traveling spouse. She believes that bringing a partner along on a business trip is generally not a good idea.

"You're always packing in every second when you're working. It doesn't matter how glamorous the location is—for me, such a trip means getting a job done well. It isn't fair to be torn between being efficient and entertaining your husband or wife. With more women executives at conferences, 'spouse programs' will have to be updated to satisfy the needs and interests of the accompanying husbands. I doubt that my spouse, who's a controller for a Minneapolis firm, would enjoy traditional afternoons of organized shopping or similar activities. I'm a firm believer that the traveling spouse-at-work should finish the job and *then* encourage his or her partner and maybe the rest of the family to fly or drive in for a spontaneous relaxing break."

Peterson, one of a handful of top executive women in the hospitality industry, has firsthand experience with the strains of being a frequently traveling parent as well as partner.

"My husband is the primary at-home care-giver. Believe me, it's an eye-opener when you've returned from several weeks on the road and find that you—the mother—are the outsider. I'm the one who has to adjust."

Radisson uses Adventure weekends to aggressively court both the family and the two-career couple who want to wind down after a week of business travel. One property, near a Six Flags amusement park, offers complimentary soft drinks in the room, family picnic baskets, and even courtesy transportation to area attractions. Many offer custom-tailored romantic packages that include a night at a local dinner theatre and other more pair-oriented inclusive options like champagne and personal keepsake photographs.

"Then there was our chocolate chip cookie coupon program," says Harriet, smiling. "Last year, when you stayed at one of our midwestern properties, we would send home a tin of fresh-baked chocolate chip cookies with a personal note. As you can imagine, that was enormously popular with business travelers."

As more women join their spouses in the ranks of frequent on-the-movers and shakers, Harriet Craig Peterson thinks that hotels will focus more on quality service and a homey atmosphere.

"We decorate with lighter color schemes and fewer pieces of 'industrial' furniture. People want their hotel rooms to have a human face and a residential feel, as well as superb service and good amenities."

She also notes that women are more likely to combine business and leisure travel. "They've really been one of the driving forces behind the 'mini-vacation.' Believe me, I can identify with that market. In fact, I believe the two-career family will really have a strong role in shaping future hotel marketing. People today are more constrained by time than money. The 'mini-vacation' provides an efficient and effective getaway."

Even luxury hotel companies like Ritz-Carlton, which has recently started a major expansion program to build properties in more resort and meeting destinations, are developing similar schemes.

Gayle B. MacIntyre, director of public relations for Ritz-Carlton, explains why the group has started its "Little Amenities" program for guests with babies and young children. "We recognize that more working couples are choosing to have children, and that those children are tomorrow's adult customers. We want them to feel at home from the beginning."

If you just can't close the loneliness gap in person (it's a bit more complicated and expensive to hop over to Japan or the Soviet Union for a quick getaway), try and develop "closeness" routines that you can practice together even when the miles seem in the millions.

Real estate developer Richard and his hotel executive

wife, Mary, play a romantic game that gets them through his increasingly frequent absences.

"When Richard travels to Europe, he calls me at least twice a day, or sends me a fax," she explains. "He tells me about some unusual site, work of art, or restaurant that he's found. Together, we begin planning a time when we'll go there together. Oddly enough, we usually do! I never get the feeling that he would rather be at those places without me—that's what really matters."

Sometimes the tug-of-travel problem can be solved with a touch of technological common sense. Writer Garvin Lally is married to entrepreneur Julie Brice, whose four-hundred-plus highly successful I Can't Believe It's Yogurt stores keep her on the move. Lally, who's currently co-authoring a book on the airline industry, has his own wanderlust, but wouldn't indulge until the pair realized that laptop computers could keep them together.

Lally grins, "That's why being married to an entreprenur is so inspirational. Julie's determination helped us to remove that entire area of stress."

Says Brice, "Garvin used to get tense because he wasn't writing. Now he can work and be with me on a much more frequent basis. One reason I'm so determined to travel right now is because we plan to have children. When that happens, I know that I'll want to be moving around a lot less than I do now."

For families with young children, staying in constant touch is even more critical. A secure toddler might not notice if Daddy or Mommy has vanished if the other parent makes a genuine effort to increase his or her time at home, but the school-age child comprehends goings and comings all too well.

"You have to do more than bring back gifts," says David, a managing engineer for a large oil firm. "You have to set the situation up positively before you depart—especially if those departures are going to happen a lot."

Let children know that you're not leaving to get away from them and your partner. Explain that this is part of your work. If they are old enough, tell them what you'll be doing while you're gone. If your son or daughter has a school project or show-and-tell that can relate to your trip, discuss what they would like you to bring back. Use maps and photographs to make your destination more tangible. To a six-year-old, North Africa or even Great Britain may seem like Saturn.

One couple, when traveling overseas, sends colorful postcards to their children, even though they may arrive home before the greetings. They find that it helps close the great distance between them.

Canadian doctor and author Peter G. Hanson believes that travel is part of today's and tomorrow's work world. "Just because one or both of you are traveling doesn't mean that your marriage and family life have to break down. There is a lot you can do. The average nontraveling couple spends fewer than twelve minutes a day conversing. Travel can actually improve communication if you make the effort. Don't let worry over hearing about domestic troubles stop you from calling home—keep the lines open."

When Hanson (whose latest book is appropriately entitled *Stress for Success*) travels—one month he logged over fifty thousand air miles—he carries along a book of children's stories. "Wherever I am, I call my kids in Toronto at their bedtime, and we have a good-night read together. Who says there's nothing valuable that you can give your kids for less than ten bucks!"

If you suspect that travel tension stems from jealousy, Dr. Hanson suggests inviting your spouse along. "Frequent-flier programs make this pretty easy on the purse. Let your husband or wife see what you actually do during a three-day jaunt to Japan. Chances are that they'll be a lot more sympathetic in the future once they see how much free time for fun you *don't* have."

When one spouse is constantly on the move, there's more than a good chance that he or she won't want to budge when vacation time rolls around. Hanson believes that honest vacation travel is an important part of a busy couple's recharging routine. "Don't just vegetate in front of the video or lie around the house. That won't really relax either of you. If your partner won't think about hopping another plane, suggest a pleasant spot that's within a half-hour drive. Business travelers must learn to separate work trips from leisure travel with their spouse or family. Think of each experience in other terms. Use a different suitcase from the one you take on business—when I take out my orange bag, I know that I'll be spending time with our kids and my wife having fun. If you cringe at sitting in cramped coach seats, concentrate on the relief of not having to drag the laptop computer along."

Above all, Hanson emphasizes the need to recognize that your spouse needs this vacation period—and so do you. Even if you're headed to the same old Charles de Gaulle airport, the Paris you'll be visiting *this* time will consist of museums, sidewalk cafés, and elegant shops—not three boardrooms.

"I generally don't recommend mixing a business trip with pleasure travel unless the business part is really minimal and won't intrude on family activities," Hanson cautions. "Never 'sabotage' a vacation with work."

As for how much or little leisure travel is beneficial to dual-career couples' sanity, Hanson has this adage: "Frequent small rewards are better than no reward." In other words, if you can only get away for a long weekend every three months, don't sit at home sulking about not having a huge chunk of travel time—get moving. You'll both feel better about life and each other in a new setting, even if the break is nothing more than a weekend package at a nearby luxury hotel. Two weeks in another town isn't always what's needed to recharge a working couple's batteries. An overnight stay in a sumptuous suite can do the trick just as well. Just make sure that the operator holds all calls until checkout time!

PARTNERS AT THE PINNACLE

Let's face it—even with the aforementioned problems, winning is still wonderful. But the two of you should have a higher aspiration than simply coming in first. You should always run to victory with an honor guard of family and friends at your side. Couples should never have to complain about "being lonely at the top."

You have each other's company for indulging and planning. Children should be front and center for any celebrations and future planning. Don't forget your parents and other close relatives who may have helped one or both of you to achieve your dreams a little faster. And friends. You'll need them most of all. Not the bartering "buddies" we've discussed in this chapter, but the men and women who care about you and your marital health. The former college roommate who straightened you out when you complained about your wife's long hours. The friendly former boss who coached you through your first national marketing presentation. Steve and Susan from next door who took your six-year-old on their annual camping trip so the two of you could catch up on some sorely needed romance. No matter how rarefied the air, you must let these folks breathe in some of your high-octane oxygen, too.

When some partners reach a summit, they start looking at each other with less than loving eyes. Your husband's style of dress and sophistication was fine for your former professional crowd, but now he's starting to make you feel uncomfortable. Maybe you've been proud of your wife's teaching skills, but is third grade an appropriate career level for a law partner's spouse? Should you have the guts to tell your beloved that his or her friends are standing in the way of country club membership? And what about her accent, his aftershave, and other previously ignored or unimportant personal traits?

Shirley Zussman has serious advice for those partners who would start nit-picking. "When a spouse feels that a current partner's looks and personality don't quite meet the new position's standards, that partner must think hard before acting or reacting. I would tell that person to look deep within him- or herself. They should examine their own insecurities. More importantly, they must ask themselves what was in the relationship before the new appointment or promotion that can be so easily discarded?"

A famous businesswoman married to an equally re-garded M.D. was about to become the first woman on the board of a major American housewares company. The final interview was to take place over dinner. The woman knew that her chances would be diminished by the fact that her husband, a Cuban refugee, still spoke with a discernible accent. They fought over whether or not he should make some excuse not to join them.

For the first time in seventeen years, the wife had to face the fact that she still harbored a tinge of prejudice and shame over her husband's background. She did not gain a seat on the board of that particular firm; she and her hus-band did gain some vital self-knowledge that salvaged their challenged relationship.

Never let success stand in the way of your love for each other. Or let it blind you to your Power Partnering responsi-bilities. Now, more than ever, is the time to reaffirm those values and feelings that prompted you to commit yourselves to mutual mentoring. Those personal commandments from the Introduction aren't just for couples starting out in the game—they're just as golden for those who've gone on to become seasoned players. Always remember the man or woman at your side who helps you reach those hard-gotten heights. His and hers laurel wreaths never go out of style—neither do partners who keep them fresh with affirmation and affection.

8

Love Means Never Having to Say "You Owe Me"

◆

All couples keep score. It's an instinctive part of the game. Who did the dishes three times last week? How much time did I spend editing your presentation? Even Power Partners are not immune to such stocktaking.

Says Lynda Robb, "There are lots of things you do. Sometimes you do them because you want to collect chits. Or you want to be a martyr. You should balance your obligations, otherwise you run the risk of one person lording it over the other."

But she, like other co-mentors we've talked with, believes that constructive score-tallying can also defuse tension. "Sometimes it's good to express your true feelings about marital debts. I ask Chuck to tell me if something really matters to him. It's always better if the gift is free—that's the best of all possible worlds. But most of us are more selfish than that. When you get married, you have to do certain things that you don't want to do. But the marriage should be more important."

Our tenth commandment of Power Partnership instructs

couples to put *themselves* before their careers. As Chrysler
Motors chief counsel Leroy Richie knows, it's not always an
easy feat.

"Things were tough," remembers Richie. "We were
standing at the train station in New Jersey. I was an associate at White & Case—Julia was working at AT&T. She was
thinking about quitting. As our commuter line pulled in, she
said, 'Roy, I think I'm going to leave my job and stay home
with the baby.' I told her that she couldn't because we
needed the money."

He continues, "She wouldn't get on the train. Julia had
tears in her eyes. She cried, 'I can't do this—you have a
support system and I don't! We can't be each other's total
means of support.' She made her decision right on that
platform."

Julia laughs. "Of course, when I was at home, the first
thing I did was become involved in getting friends together
and starting my own company, Minority Manufacturing.
The point is that Roy gave me that option."

A short time later, Julia began what looked like a promising career in New Jersey politics. Suddenly, her husband
was offered the plum position at Chrysler. "I asked her to
drop a local election campaign to move with me to Detroit,"
says Leroy Richie, who admits that he was, and still is,
somewhat uncomfortable with his wife's impulse for a public career.

Recalls Julia, "I needed to have Roy with me when I was
on the stump. He would help me like crazy in the background, but not when I was center stage. Ironically, it was
his idea that I should run for City Council."

"I had a female friend," says Leroy. "She really helped
me through my problems with Julia's going public. I know
that if we stay in the Detroit area, she'll be running for
mayor of our town. Of the two of us, she's the one with the
potential to be a real mover and shaker. I've learned that
I'm not always the best judge of what she's saying in a public
forum. There have been times when I've been horrified by
her frankness. At the same time, I have more confidence in

her—she's one of the straightest and most moral human beings I've ever known. If I have a serious judgment call in my work, I will know what to do if I consult with Julia."

The Richies are not alone when it comes to dealing successfully with the give-and-take of dual-career married life. Gail and Scott Fosler are a couple who've found that security can spring from giving each other the right to professional satisfaction, even if it means two households and a weekly commute between New York and Washington, D.C.

Gail is the chief economist and executive director of the Conference Board, one of this country's best-known research organizations dealing with workplace and economic issues, while her husband is vice president and director of government programs for the Committee for Economic Development. Each had been previously married; together, they are helping to raise Scott's teenage son.

"So many people were shocked that I chose to accept a position that would take me away from my husband and stepson," Gail says. "I had to keep telling them that this wasn't a snap decision that I made on my own. Scott and I had many long talks about my working in Manhattan. His son is in college, and all three of us like New York. In fact, there are many events of mine that Scott would pass by if they were in D.C.—he goes with me more frequently now that I'm in another city. All of us make much more effort to spend time together. Scott knows that the Conference Board position is a job that I really love, just as I know that his current occupation is special to him."

Hattie Winston and Harold Wheeler have also learned how to compromise without resentment. "Partnership has so many different domains," stresses Harold. "Once, Hattie was up for a TV series at the same time that I was scoring a film for Disney. If we had needed to move to Los Angeles, it would have meant a major career sacrifice for me. We talked about it. In the end, I was willing to make the move if necessary, because I realized that Hattie had been making career adjustments for me all along. We had never talked about this problem before."

Adds Hattie, "Sometimes in a marriage, you're both so busy with all of your roles that you forget how to be a couple. Work and parenthood can be *so* serious! Husbands and wives have to give themselves a chance to be playful again."

As if to prove that point, the couple has written an as-yet-unpublished song entitled, "Love Is Two People Being Extremely Selfish Together."

POWER HOUSES WITH HEART

Screen characters Oliver and Barbara Rose gave togetherness a deadly twist in Danny DeVito's controversial dark comedy, *The War of the Roses*. This film fable about a married couple's battle over their possession-laden dream house shows what happens when partnership diminishes instead of grows with financial and social success.

DeVito, co-starring as the divorce lawyer who has learned the value of marital mentoring, takes the audience on a *Christmas Carol*–style trip back in time to the beginnings of the relationship. We see stars Michael Douglas and Kathleen Turner in the heat of passionate romance, starting out with humble surroundings but rich in determination and affection. As the pair rises in Washington, D.C., society, we watch each become more obsessed with his or her own agenda.

When Turner goes back to work, Douglas suffers a loss of self-esteem. Instead of bolstering his confidence, she digs in with a vengeance, repaying him for earlier public embarrassments he had put her through in the name of success. Eventually, the pair decide to divorce, but end up living together because they refuse to give up the house. But how much importance can a piece of real estate have for a couple who would rather not even live together?

Anyone who has seen the film knows the grim, improbable outcome. Who could feel such love in the beginning of a marriage, and then go on to do what they do to each other and those around them? (Ironically, their two children have turned out reasonably sane and loving, a testament to the fact that each has the capacity to care.)

Fox Television commentator Judy Licht knows all too well how even the most dedicated couples can come close to walking on the identical knife's edge. "Jerry and I have had some very bad times," she admits. "There have been three particularly terrible periods—*always about houses!* Fights over real estate are really about power. Where and how you live is a major life decision. So much time and money is tied up in houses. With us, kids, sex, and work are just fine. Some couples fight over one of those areas." (Interestingly enough, during his separate interview, husband Jerry Della Femina spoke glowingly about how Judy could always make even the smallest living space "sexy.")

Licht continues, "Those times are depressing because we're both so strong-willed. We feel trapped. I think that Jerry is still a dirty fighter—we're both manipulators. What's devastating is that there's no alternative for us except to get through these times and move on. I know that Jerry is the only man I could ever be married to at this point in my life. In a way, it's positive. We don't give each other or ourselves any alternative. Either we'll make it or end up alone and miserable."

Della Femina concurred. "When it's good, it's great. When we argue, it's terrible. We can't leave, so we fight hard."

But this real-life couple has learned Power Partnership's most vital lesson—that the true teamwork marriage has the strength to survive those temporary though seemingly devastating frictions. Bad times *can* happen to good couples. The point is to recognize how the two of you are more important than the downside moment at hand. In the same two interviews, Licht and Della Femina also had this to say about their relationship:

"Being alone out there is hard. I don't know how people do it," says the world-famous advertising mogul. "If you're not part of a team—it's terrible. Judy and I get off on each other's accomplishments. It makes having power fun. I have more fun watching Judy win than winning myself. She feels the same way. If you look at yourselves this way, what do you give up? You give up loneliness and not having someone around to bounce ideas off of."

He recalls a recent emotional epiphany. "Coming back from our house in the Hamptons—three and a half hours on the road at night. The baby was cutting a tooth. Our four-year-old had a cold and was crying her head off. Both of our dogs wouldn't stop barking. Judy and I were laughing like kids. This was our life and wasn't it great! Many people would look on such a situation as a minor disaster. Not us. We crawled back on Route 27 and the Long Island Expressway at ten miles per hour—holding hands the entire way."

Judy describes the way she sees their activity-packed marriage of nearly eight years. "We think of ourselves in terms of a basketball team. We're players who constantly switch off and carry the ball for each other. If one of us has a weakness in a given situation, the other steps in with his or her strength. That's what good teammates do—one comes in with a burst of speed when the other falters. Neither of us could do this with our former spouses. Meeting each other was a liberating experience."

About owing each other, Licht adds knowingly, "When you really love someone, doing favors for each other is quid pro quo . . . but you can't keep score. What you *know* each of you has is someone who adores you—that's where you find solace. A real house, a real family, and a person who gives you genuine support. If something outside those three things hurts you, having that solidity helps."

As Licht and Della Femina told us, sex is not necessarily the frontline vulnerability of today's two-career marriages. Jennifer Knopf, co-director of Northwestern University's Sex Therapy and Education Program, recently shared her findings with the *Austin American-Statesman*. She wanted to see who among advanced-degree-holding professional couples had the better sex lives. Knopf believes her most important

finding was that there did not seem to be any direct correla-
tion between the number of hours a couple worked and the
quality or frequency of the sex they had.

"In certain circumstances, more work was associated
with better sex," says Knopf. "As a clinician, what I came to
understand was [that what was important was] the marriage's ability to respond to stress rather than the stress
itself."

Psychology Today recently released a random sample
Gallup poll, commissioned by the publication, along with
King World's "Inside Edition" and ABC's "HOME." This
study showed that most American couples are committed to
their marriages, and work hard at maintaining their sexual
fidelity. Ironically, many of these same pairs didn't see
themselves and their behavior as the norm. The survey went
on to demonstrate that we're still a highly monogamous
nation, filled with spouses who see each other as both "best
friends" and "mysterious, exciting and skillful lovers."

These couples revealed that they were willing to work
"very hard" to keep romance a vital component of their
relationships. They also gave substance to the study's revelation that partners who engage in regular religious worship
express more passion for each other.

CHANGING PARTNERS AND PERCEPTIONS

Throughout this book, we've talked about teamwork on
many levels—practical, tactical, and emotional. Just as various sports require a repertoire of cooperative moves, so
marital teamwork and co-mentoring must develop variety
and flexibility with an eye toward the future.

Gail Fosler's work at the Conference Board, along with
her own experiences as a dual-career marital partner, has
led her to these observations about why the Power Partner
approach will become more natural as we head into the next
century.

"There is a much more inherently egalitarian attitude
between younger couples," observes Fosler. "As I look back

five or ten years in the demographic spectrum, the whole aspect of running the home and child-rearing seems to have changed."

Those of us in our twenties and thirties find sharing the load and throwing out scorecards easier than do those a mere half generation ahead. "Men in their forties and fifties are the ones who have had to adapt the most," Fosler believes.

She recalls an incident that brought this fact into focus. "Back in the early 1970s, I was working as an economist for a major bank. Whenever there was a meeting, my (fiftyish) boss would direct me, the only woman, to set up the room, get the coffee, and make sure that everyone had notepads, etc. I finally confronted him about my resentment at being singled out for these 'female' chores. At first, he told me that I had to control myself if I wanted to get ahead. But later, he called me back to his office.

" 'Gail,' he said, 'I took a good look at a photograph of my five daughters and thought about what you said. You're right. That's not what I want for them.' He has since become one of my strongest advocates."

Most of our married co-mentors agree that public perceptions will change, albeit slowly, to meet the needs of those partners whose marital expectations go beyond the nightly call of "Honey, I'm home!" Bard College president Leon Botstein thinks that a woman has "unequal needs that have to be met in order for her to succeed at her career and in raising children." He adds, "It should get easier as two-career living becomes more common. The approach makes more sense as we live longer."

His wife, curator Barbara Haskell, adds, "It will be the only world available—true partnership will be the only option—the next stage has to allow more flexibility."

Bryn Mawr's director of public information, Debra J. Thomas, agrees that people will change business, and business will change society.

"The expectation is there. The students I talk with anticipate full-time careers and families. Then I ask them if the men in their lives are more supportive and egalitarian. The answer is usually no. That's the biggest hurdle—most men still want women to meet their expectations in social and sexual terms, second paycheck or not. On the positive side, many of these men, even at the dating stage, are more accepting of the fact that the women in their lives will be working as intensely as themselves."

Thomas continues, "The greatest reason for optimism is the shortage of skilled people in the workplace. In order to woo and keep the best talent, companies will be forced to change their outlooks. My husband and I have always approached marriage as a team effort. The more of us there are in the professional world, the more pressure will be brought to bear on institutions and corporations. When these changes become commonplace, society will then accept them as part of the 'system.' "

Donna Karan thinks that her children will benefit simply by being raised in a dual-career home. "They will be experienced with the situation and will be able to handle any difficulties and questions that might come up more smoothly. There will be less of a mother-at-home expectation in their adult lifetimes."

Elizabeth Dole's opinions about the future of two-career families echoes these sentiments. "Helping to ensure that work and family are complementary and not conflicting goals is a priority of mine as secretary of labor. There are both demands and rewards that result from two-career families. Certainly, one of the benefits is that each partner is able to empathize with the tugs and pulls."

Dole predicts, like Debra Thomas and others, that companies will have to rethink their policies. "America's labor force is growing at only 1 percent annually, its slowest rate in forty years. This slow growth is expected to continue for the rest of the century. Employers are learning that one of the best ways to recruit and retain employees is to be responsive to the needs of employees, whether it be providing child care, parental leave, flexible work schedules, or flexible benefit packages.

"At the Department of Labor, we have established a Work and Family Clearinghouse, designed to assist employers in identifying policies and programs that have succeeded in meeting the child care needs of employees. Anyone can call toll-free at 1-800-827-5335."

Co-preneurs Jacky and Jeff Clyman and Joan and David Helpern acknowledge that some of the myths die hard—especially traditional expectations about the role of women. Says Jacky, "Jeff comes from a traditional home. He was brought up to believe that when a woman is assertive, she's a ball-buster. It took him a while to see the difference."

"Seeing Jacky and other women taking the lead did make me uncomfortable," Jeff concedes.

David Helpern, a more senior Power Partner, has always accepted Joan's professional drive. "Couples have to make some basic decisions as mates and parents. If a woman is miserable at home, she's going to make their children unhappy."

Adds the ever-involved Joan, "All focus does not revolve around my kids . . . which is good. In this kind of a marriage, you're always stressed and tired. So what? You're more interesting and fulfilled."

Barbara Walters insists that it takes an effort on each mate's behalf to keep the ball in motion. "I'm always asked if it's possible for a woman to have a *great* career, marriage, and children. You can only do it when you've got your spouse's support—which I have."

Ashford & Simpson constantly strive to maintain their marital equilibrium—in spite of their long relationship and spiritual bond to their music and each other. Says Nick, "I wrote a song called 'How Does It Fit?' I hear more and more that powerful women don't want men. It gives me thoughts about Val and myself."

He continues, "I think relationships will be tougher because the structure of society is changing. Women are changing. Even the way I write songs now is different. I used to write simpler lyrics. Women's independence has changed that. Adjusting to Val's being a career woman took major changing in my thinking."

Valerie sighs. "I'm not sure that I reassure him, but I know I need him. If a woman is successful, there's always going to be a tinge of envy. As much as I want Nick's success, I'll be jealous, too. But we talk about it even though it may be a pain. You both have to accept it."

Nick feels that men must express their needs. "You have to reassure *yourself*, but men want reinforcement, too—the way a man tells a woman that she looks good or did something well. You have to respect each other as individuals. Sometimes you can't settle problems—you both have to rely on your commitment."

Which is precisely what Power Partnership is all about—commitment without unspoken limits or hidden agendas. Accepting and embracing each other's enjoyment of work, child-rearing, and social activity. Having an understanding that no one else can quite comprehend . . . even your oldest friends and family members.

Lauren and Michael Falk, the young couple whose individual entrepreneurial careers in trade publishing and marketing bring them into frequent co-mentoring contact, reflect how working partners coming up through the ranks have artlessly absorbed what more mature couples have arrived at through quiet acts of emotional and psychological boldness.

Says Lauren, "We can't share a lot of our life with our families because they don't understand what we have. Some of our siblings are actually envious of how we operate. My sister was working for Michael. At one point, I found a mistake in something she did. In her anger, she blurted out how hard Michael worked for me and that I should be grateful. I told her that Michael and I *always* do the best for each other—we don't keep score. We're too proud of one another to do anything but give what's needed to get the job done well."

Michael smiles. "We spend a lot of time working because, for us, it's a blast. There aren't any whip marks on my back."

This commitment has gotten the Falks through some less-than-wonderful work times that could have created a lasting rift. "Michael once gave me direct mail advice that really bombed. I just realized that it was part of the learning curve. Better that he lost my company's money than that of his own clients. We were lucky enough to learn a business lesson without jeopardizing our futures," explains Lauren matter-of-factly.

Stockbroker-turned-entrepreneur Ludwig Gelobter talks about the time that he thought about getting into his wife's world. "Before she went into business and communications, Barbara was a highly paid singer. I thought that artist management would be my next career move. I was not a great success, although I did meet some great people. Barbara let me give it a try. We've always been open to each other's efforts. It's not a contract. I took care of the kids while she was on the road and off in Nigeria. By the same token, when I became heavily involved in New York politics, she supported my efforts. We've always had our commitment tested. My parents weren't thrilled about our marriage until the children came. In 1959, we had trouble getting good apartments because of our different races. Even today, we're aware of these problems."

ROOM TO MOVE—CO-MENTORING IN MOTION

Stephen and Fredrica Friedman sum up strong partnership with this succinct phrase: "What creates a successful marriage is successful accommodation."

Dr. Shirley Zussman goes a step further. "Partners should be able to have separate lives within their joint relationship. This can manifest itself through work or leisure-time interests. It can also come to the fore through differences of opinion and approach. This 'separateness' can bring a couple much closer than fear of abandonment. Women, especially, used to have more dependency because society taught them that they needed a man around to survive. Now we know that this isn't the best emotional pattern for women . . . or men."

She stresses the importance for each mate to stand on his or her own two feet, and be unafraid to assert individuality. "Being together should reinforce each spouse's self-image rather than submerging those different qualities.

"A perfect example of this is the partner who says, 'Maybe we can go to the movies tonight,' instead of 'I'd like to see that new film with Tom Hanks.' Couples must be able to thrive and grow as separate entities within their union."

Zussman admits, however, that assertiveness continues to be overtaken by the mutual yearning to be cared for. "Perhaps those who are starting their marriages now will find it easier to strike the right balance between psychological self-reliance and merging. Couples shouldn't concentrate on completing each other. At the same time, they shouldn't hold work satisfaction in higher esteem than the pleasure gained from intimacy—sexual and emotional—with their mate."

Caring and being cared for is rapidly becoming an emerging theme for the 1990s. Harriet Craig Peterson talks about how this phenomenon is already being felt in the hospitality industry. "At Radisson, we instituted an employee program called Yes-I-Can. This was designed to help staff better anticipate the needs of hotel guests. Now, we're changing the name to Yes-I-Care. This reflects the desire for nurturing which everyone, especially working couples, will look for during their leisure breaks."

Peterson contends, "When these career couples travel, especially when they're combining the professional with the personal, they'll seek out those facilities which reflect their own feelings. Places that are comforting and caring as well as stylish and state-of-the-art will have the edge. If you've only got two or three days to catch your breath and 'rediscover' each other, you'll trade up for the more conducive atmosphere."

Both the Bureau of Labor Statistics and the Conference

Board's findings indicate that the age of the two-career family is well upon us. Says Gail Fosler, "By the year 2000, two-thirds of the labor force will consist of two-income couples. And . . . two-thirds of *those* partners will be parents! That's a big jump from the beginning of the 1980s."

The most rapid two-career couple growth areas are in sales and technology. Cites Fosler, "In 1983, only 42 percent of two-income couples worked in those fields; today's figure is around 65 percent. This includes careers in management and communications, too."

Maybe this ties in with Dr. Ann Curtain Ward's contention that media mothers are more in touch with their offspring than other professionals because of their relative ease at humanizing modern communications equipment. And don't forget the couple who fax nightly "sweet nothings" to each other during business trips. But as we have demonstrated, hardware alone is no substitute for innovative marital attitudes.

UP WHERE WE BELONG

John and Ellie Raynolds' 1989 Christmas card featured a photograph of themselves in identical hiking gear, pointing in opposite directions on a rugged mountaintop. The holiday greeting closed with this ironic rejoinder: "Two Career Couple Coordinates in Everything."

Here is the ideal Power Partnering stance: one team headed up the hill, but secure enough to seek out separate paths along the way. Determined to reach the summit, but not at the cost of losing what you've gained during the climb.

Couples who maintain strong individual goals and identities while giving each other unconditional support could turn out to be the healthiest. We've eschewed the promise "to obey" in the traditional marriage vows; a good substitute might be the pledge to inspire. That is what the partners in this book seem to do best. Whether it be encouraging your mate to publish a novel, lose thirty pounds, or run for office, the act of unconscious inspiration makes the difference.

Power Partnership doesn't end with a couple's achieving its goals. It endures beyond success, into the years when the glory of accomplishment can fade. If spouses have not fully come to terms with one another, when the victories come fewer and farther between, they may be left with little self-esteem.

Men and women who fall in love and commit themselves to building up each partner's strengths don't suffer ego loss as deeply. They develop inner emotional resources founded upon their spouse's trust and respect. When a career starts to flag or a business doesn't meet the bottom line, one can still say, "I believe in this—*she's* behind me, too, so let's think about what step *we* should take next." No matter if the other is not actually there in the flesh; co-mentoring can and should become a state of mind and heart.

That degree of purpose requires Power Partnership. As we have seen, the changes do not come overnight. Relationships take time to reveal their true natures and priorities. Which is why we've placed so much emphasis on knowing what goals you wish for yourself, your mate and your marriage.

Throughout the 1990s and beyond, staying together will become more of a challenge even as it increases in desirability. Choices will not disappear, although the gulf between what's acceptable and preferable may widen.

Letitia Baldrige, a firm believer in the institution of marriage, says, "As more Berlin Walls come tumbling down, so will marriages. Yet marriage is the last rock to cling to on this earth. The more our lives change, the more we should make an effort to keep couples and families together."

Few of us see marriage in terms of a test. Yet couples are constantly under challenge—by the pressures of the workplace, the media, the law, and even the environment. When a company relocates, or if a family home is struck by lightning or blown away by a tornado, teamwork must come before passion. If legislation does not provide, marital trust and communication has to take up the slack. Thanks to loopholes in public insurance policy, couples have actually needed to legally separate to ensure one or both adequate health care during the later years of life! Legislators are working to change these, just as more enlightened corporations and firms are discarding restrictions concerning married co-workers and inflexible time clocks.

Power Partnering does not always guarantee an A or even a B-plus on the marital exam. Sometimes co-mentoring isn't enough to prevent the worst—or even second worst—from occurring. Those ten commandments won't keep the tire from puncturing on the morning of the presentation or the afternoon of the high school ice skating finals. They will not ensure a life free from arguments or an occasional night of less than blissful sex. Nor will they serve as a blueprint for becoming surefire co-preneurs.

Joyce and Ted Rice, along with our other Power Partners, know that marriage, like business, is a series of attempts. Not all will succeed, but as Joyce says of their relationship and company, T. J. Cinnamons, "No one can take away your trying." Co-mentoring makes the trying more worthwhile.

Being a Power Partner to your spouse ultimately means being one to yourself. As each of you builds the other's confidence, your own identity will become clearer. By being open and caring with your mate, you'll gain invaluable insight into your own feelings and motivations. Change will feel less unsettling; setbacks less frustrating. Even when you don't come in first, you will always be part of a winning team because both of you are playing for keeps.

INDEX

ABOUT THE AUTHORS

Jane Hershey Cuozzo is a New York–based writer and editor. Her articles have appeared in *Good Housekeeping, US, Family Weekly, Being Well, American Film,* Northwestern Mutual Life's *Creative Living,* and *The American Journal of Psychoanalysis.* She is a longtime contributor to Fodor's Travel Publications and is a contributing editor to *Hollywood Magazine.*

Cuozzo is a summa cum laude graduate of the University of Pennsylvania and a member of Phi Beta Kappa. She was the recipient of a Thouron Scholarship for study in Great Britain, where she received a Higher Diploma in Film at the University of London. Her Power Partner is *New York Post* assistant managing editor Steve Cuozzo.

S. Diane Graham is president and CEO of STRATCO, a fast-growing international chemical engineering company based in Kansas City. She is a member of the Committee of 200. Graham is married to co-preneur Terry Robertson, a chemical engineer, who is executive vice president of STRATCO. Robertson is the father of two college-age sons, and together the couple has four children.

Graham has degrees in business and economics from Culver-Stockton College and from the Harvard Business School's Owner/President Management Program. She has been featured on the cover of *Nation's Business* and has appeared on numerous radio talk shows.

OTHER MASTERMEDIA BOOKS

THE PREGNANCY AND MOTHERHOOD DIARY: Planning the First Year of Your Second Career, by Susan Schiffer Stautberg, is the first and only undated appointment diary that shows how to manage pregnancy and career. ($12.95 spiralbound)

CITIES OF OPPORTUNITY: Finding the Best Place to Work, Live and Prosper in the 1990's and Beyond, by Dr. John Tepper Marlin, explores the job and living options for the next decade and into the next century. This consumer guide and handbook, written by one of the world's experts on cities, selects and features forty-six American cities and metropolitan areas. ($13.95 paper, $24.95 cloth)

THE DOLLARS AND SENSE OF DIVORCE, by Judith Briles, is the first book to combine practical tips on overcoming the legal hurdles with planning before, during, and after divorce. ($10.95 paper)

OUT THE ORGANIZATION: How Fast Could You Find a New Job?, by Madeleine and Robert Swain, is written for the millions of Americans whose jobs are no longer safe, whose companies are not loyal, and who face futures of uncertainty. It gives advice on finding a new job or starting your own business. ($11.95 paper, $17.95 cloth)

AGING PARENTS AND YOU: A Complete Handbook to Help You Help Your Elders Maintain a Healthy, Productive and Independent Life, by Eugenia Anderson-Ellis and Marsha Dryan, is a complete guide to providing care to aging relatives. It gives practical advice and resources to the adults who are helping their elders lead productive and independent lives. ($9.95 paper)

CRITICISM IN YOUR LIFE: How to Give It, How to Take It, How to Make It Work for You, by Dr. Deborah Bright, offers practical advice, in an upbeat, readable, and realistic fashion, for turning criticism into control. Charts and diagrams guide the reader into managing criticism from bosses, spouses, children, friends, neighbors, and in-laws. ($9.95 paper, $17.95 cloth)

BEYOND SUCCESS: How Volunteer Service Can Help You Begin Making a Life Instead of Just a Living, by John F. Raynolds III and Eleanor Raynolds, C.B.E., is a unique how-to book targeted to business and professional people considering volunteer work, senior citizens who wish to fill leisure time meaningfully, and students trying out various career options. The book is filled with interviews with celebrities, CEOs, and average citizens who talk about the benefits of service work. ($9.95 paper, $19.95 cloth)

MANAGING IT ALL: Time-Saving Ideas for Career, Family, Relationships and Self, by Beverly Benz Treuille and Susan Schiffer Stautberg, is written for women who are juggling careers and families. Over two hundred career women (ranging from a TV anchorwoman to an investment banker) were interviewed. The book contains many humorous anecdotes on saving time and improving the quality of life for self and family. ($9.95 paper)

REAL LIFE 101: (Almost) Surviving Your First Year Out of College, by Susan Kleinman, supplies welcome advice to those facing "real life" for the first time, focusing on work, money, health, and how to deal with freedom and responsibility. ($9.95 paper)

YOUR HEALTHY BODY, YOUR HEALTHY LIFE: How to Take Control of Your Medical Destiny, by Donald B. Louria, M.D., provides precise advice and strategies that will help you to live a long and healthy life. Learn also about nutrition, exercise, vitamins, and medication, as well as how to control risk factors for major diseases. ($12.95 paper)

THE CONFIDENCE FACTOR: How Self-Esteem Can Change Your Life, by Judith Briles, is based on a nationwide survey of six thousand men and women. Briles explores why women so often feel a lack of self-confidence and have a poor opinion of themselves. She offers step-by-step advice on becoming the person you want to be. ($18.95 cloth)

THE SOLUTION TO POLLUTION: 101 Things You Can Do to Clean Up Your Environment, by Laurence Sombke, offers step-by-step techniques on how to conserve more energy, start a recycling center, choose biodegradable products, and proceed with individual environmental cleanup projects. ($7.95 paper)

TAKING CONTROL OF YOUR LIFE: The Secrets of Successful Enterprising Women, by Gail Blanke and Kathleen Walas, is based on the authors' professional experience with Avon Products' Women of Enterprise Awards, given each year to outstanding women entrepreneurs. The authors offer a specific plan to help you gain control over your life and include business tips and quizzes as well as beauty and lifestyle information. ($17.95 cloth)

Life on the fast track is too tough to go it alone anymore, and two-career couples are learning the important difference between being competitors and being Power Partners. Today's dual-income relationships offer couples a unique opportunity to help each other win at work without losing at home. *Power Partners* explores these relationships and suggests some important ground rules for making them work.

You will discover men and women who have made the conscious decision to do more for their mates than simply cheer from the sidelines. Among the couples featured are Robert and Elizabeth Dole, Donna Karan and Stephan Weiss, Hattie Winston and Harold Wheeler, Judy Licht and Jerry Della Femina, Joan and David Helpern, Angela and Bruce Cummings, Senator Charles Robb and Lynda Johnson Robb, Nick Ashford and Valerie Simpson, Congresswoman Pat Schroeder and Jim Schroeder, Bob Bradford and Barbara Taylor Bradford, as well as experts such as etiquette authority Letitia Baldrige and marital therapist Dr. Shirley Zussman.

The book, which is upbeat and positive, includes interactive quizzes to play with your partner and covers the danger signals that can come with prosperity, the way to establish a regular co-mentoring routine, applying professional networking techniques to your own situation, the hidden power of family life, and the dos and don'ts of powerful home entertaining when mixing business and friendship.